Stay Inside

Victoria Olsen

Copyright © 2024 by Victoria Olsen

All rights reserved.

No portion of this book may be reproduced in any form without written permission from the publisher or author, except as permitted by U.S. copyright law.

Contents

1. Foreword — 1
2. 1. Lothryn — 3
3. 2. Hannah — 10
4. 3. Lothryn — 16
5. 4. Hannah — 22
6. 5. Lothryn — 28
7. 6. Hannah — 34
8. 7. Lothryn — 41
9. 8. Hannah — 48
10. 9. Lothryn — 55
11. 10. Hannah — 60
12. 11. Lothryn — 65
13. 12. Hannah — 70
14. 13. Lothryn — 74
15. 14. Hannah — 79

16.	15. Lothryn	85
17.	16. Hannah	89
18.	17. Lothryn	95
19.	18. Hannah	99
20.	19. Lothryn	105
21.	20. Hannah	110
22.	21. Lothryn	118
23.	22. Hannah	125
24.	23. Lothryn	133
25.	24. Hannah	139
26.	25. Lothryn	147
27.	26. Hannah	152
28.	27. Lothryn	159
29.	28. Hannah	166
30.	29. Lothryn	175
31.	30. Hannah	182
32.	00. David	190

Foreword

For Branwyne

Sometimes movies don't get finished.

It's sad, but it's true. Creating a film is an incredible endeavor that happens in approximately four stages: Preproduction, Production, Post-Production, and Selling/Marketing/Festival Submission. In my opinion, Only the first two stages are fun. Preproduction involves writing, casting, planning, location hunting, etc. It's a period full of hope and excitement. The actual production is a filled with a similar electricity. Most everyone who works on a movie set will agree to the old adage- It's the best business I know.

When I was twenty-six, I set out to make a movie called Stay Inside on a budget of approximately $20,000. That's lower than low budget. But everyone was thrilled to work on it and I was willing to put myself into credit card debt to make it happen. I sent my script around to various agents in an attempt to secure some sort of recognizable name talent which would help the funding I the long run. The agents read my script and returned to me with glowing reviews. One even said that it was the best script that had ever been across her desk. I was on cloud nine. But I still couldn't secure enough funding and I had to shoot the film non-union.

Luckily, my cast of non-union talent was incredible. They poured their hearts and souls into their performances and made the dialogue shine. We all felt like we came together to make something special.

But this story ended in post-production. Promises weren't kept, agreements weren't honored. Editing and mastering is an intensive labor for someone uninvested in a project. It requires a studied set of skills I've never had the temperament to master. I've never had the money to pay a third party to edit the footage, to color, to add sfx, to give the film the TLC it deserves. And so it sits in a hard drive.

I have carried the guilt of this unfinished project for years. I'm deeply sorry to the cast and crew who loved this story as much as me. I'm sorry to the friends and family I let down.

I decided only recently to convert this screenplay into a novel so that it may live in some form. I've discovered as I am writing that the act is sometimes therapeutic and other times traumatic.

I've also learned it's generally tricky to turn a dual-protagonist screenplay into a dual-protagonist novel. But after some thought, I decided that switching between the first person perspectives of both Lothryn and Hannah would be the most effective way to tell this cerebral tale that is so dependent upon how each character experiences the events of the story.

There are many lessons to learn from failure and what we learn helps us move on. I do wish for one day to see this story completed as a film- either as the original footage or in the hands of a larger budget taking it on anew. Until then, I hope this novel exudes the same level of intrigue, emotion, and electricity that I felt on set years ago.

-Paul Bianchi

1. Lothryn

My father was my entire world.

That isn't an exaggeration. He was the only person I interacted with until I was seventeen years old. I had never left our apartment. I had never been outside. My skin was untouched by the sun, barring the gentle kisses of light that spilled through our boarded-up windows. I was pale and malnourished, skinnier than I wanted to be. But that was to be expected in post-apocalyptic life, or so I was told.

He said my mother had named me Lothryn. I had no idea my name was unusual; I had nothing to compare it to. My father had an unusual name as well. He was called Eramice by no one. I only called him "dad" and there were no other living humans around to use his first name.

Dad said he never found any other survivors like us. We lived in what was once a great city. He said there used to be decent living people, families in every home. It was too crowded, a city of lights and entertainment and dreams. But not anymore.

The streets were crawling with the victims, however. They were zombies. A lab-created virus had swept across the world. What began as a simple respiratory disease, progressed into a violent half-death. The populace became soulless fiends that preyed upon living flesh. They were vicious monsters and Dad made certain I knew to fear them. He said they dripped black blood from rotting faces. They were unnaturally strong and could chew through bones.

As I got older, I was less fearful and mostly interested. I had never seen one in person. Occasionally I would hear sounds from outside, mechanical remnants of society, the bark of an undead dog, or the scream of a zombie. But they were horrors for my father to face alone when he left our home to scavenge for food and supplies. I was never allowed to go with him.

I always hoped he would take me along. I wanted him to believe that I was grown-up enough to protect myself. With every passing birthday, I would ask him if I was old enough to go outside with him.

"Maybe, next year," he would respond.

I thought for sure that on my seventeenth birthday, he would finally say yes. He had made comments on my physique in the months prior. He noticed that I was getting taller and stronger. I wasn't the pathetic bean pole I was at fifteen. I had hair under my arms and on my legs. Dad taught me how to shave my moustache and the patchy bristles on my chin.

But I was also afraid to ask him. I didn't want to hear him say no again. Dad could be quite intimidating when he wanted to be. He wasn't especially tall or muscular. I was already nearly his height and likely his weight. But he had a commanding voice and wild eyes that convinced me on more than one occasion that the world had claimed at least a portion of his sanity. He was mostly soft-spoken, so it was jarring any time he raised his voice. I, on the other hand, had my share of tantrums; the consequence of which meant raising my voice was less intimidating and more expected.

He said he happened upon a treat for me that birthday, a cake from a place he called a drugstore down the road. He assured me that it was one of the many foods so filled with fat and preservatives that it was safe to eat far beyond its expiration date. He called it a Twinkie, which delighted me to no end. It came in a clear plastic wrapper and was shaped like a phallus. He stuck a small blue candle in the sweet golden sponge, lit it with a lighter, and told me to make a birthday wish.

I was so tired of being stuck indoors. I wanted desperately for there to be a change. I wished broadly for something to change my world. In the moment, I didn't care how it happened. I wanted the zombies in our city to finally succumb to their deaths. I wanted my father to trust me enough to take me out into the world. I wanted another survivor to show up on my door step, preferably a beautiful woman like the ones I found in the pages of old magazines. I wanted to touch a breast. My wish was utterly selfish, but I extinguished the flame anyway.

I licked the cream from the end of the candle. It was deliciously sweet, an incredible rare treat. At a younger age, I might've been pacified by its sweetness. I might have instantly forgotten about my desires as I indulged in the euphoria of sugar. But I needed my father to know my wish. I wanted him in his happiest of moods for when I voiced my wish.

"Tell the story again- about how the world fell away into ruin," I asked him.

Dad's eyes twinkled in the dim candlelight. In a kinder world, my dad would have been a famous storyteller. He loved to weave a tale with rich details and I loved to listen. He was never happier than when he was orating to me, his adoring captive audience.

"I must've told you that story a hundred times," he said with a chuckle.

"I know," I said. I feigned embarrassment. "It's just that I like to hear the story from time to time. And I'm seventeen now. I know you've been leaving out some gory details."

"In places."

That much was true. All my life, it was a story that had grown in length and specifics. I felt like every time I heard it, I learned something new about my father, my mother and the world that used to be.

From what I understood, there was some shadowy organization, a secret branch of the former government. They created a virus in a lab. They were trying to reanimate corpses and use them as cheap military or labor. My mother used to work for them until she discovered the evil that was being done behind closed doors. Her name was Sallas. She told my father. Together they tried to warn the rest of the world, but they were caught.

"Those awful people held us against our will," my father told me. "Your mother was a brilliant scientist. I was a chemist. We worked around the clock to develop an antidote to the deadly virus. But we knew as soon as we told them the formula, they would have us killed."

My parents were interrogated for hours, but they refused to give them the formula. Then all too suddenly, the virus breached the confines of the lab. Zombies poured through the hallways tearing apart and infecting the living. It quickly spread outwards, the most violent plague the world had ever seen. My father managed to escape the facility with a tray of his antidote. My mother was less fortunate.

"Now, if you ever find yourself in this situation, you have to remember two things," he warned me. "Never let anyone fall behind and always watch the stairs."

That's how the zombies got her. One grabbed her ankle and tripped her as they ran up the stairs. There was nothing he could do to save her. My father watched the zombies tear her apart before his eyes.

"I loved your mother so much," he said. "But, I had to live for you, buddy. By the time I made it back to you, the world was well on its way to becoming what it is today. Overrun by those flesh eaters, the dashed hopes, and liars. But what's truth anyway?" he liked to add. "The world exists only how we see it from our individual perspectives."

There was a time that hearing about my mother's death would upset me. But the more I heard the story, it became less impactful. Or maybe less real. I never knew my mother, but I saw her as this impossibly noble warrior, a brilliant mind, a champion for truth and justice who lost her life fighting the good fight.

Sometimes my father would tell parts of the story in the language of the old world. "English" I heard him call it sometimes. I knew it was written on the packs of food he would bring home, or in the magazines and newspapers that browned with age on our shelves. I asked him if he would let me learn to speak and read it as well as he could.

"It's the language of savages, Lothryn," He assured me. "It's not worth it."

The language we spoke was more simple and elegant. Semaj-Kire, it was called, the language of enlightened survivors. I still wanted to learn English. I wanted to read.

He studied my face after telling me the story. I was used to this behavior. Sometimes he would look at me with overwhelming pride and love. His eyes would tear up at the corners and he would tell me sweetly, "I can't believe I created you." Other times, he'd become saddened and withdrawn. I'd assume my face reminded him of my mother. I could sense guilt, perhaps for leaving her behind.

I was so lucky to have him, I thought. I never once doubted he loved me.

"I know what you're about to ask me," he said.

"How?"

I licked the sweet cream from my fingers pensively. My heart started to race. How could I have been so transparent?

"Because you ask me every year," he replied.

He stood and paced around our grim living room. He had lit several candles. His shadow danced upon the tattered quilts that hung upon our walls, quilts that muffled our noise so as not to attract a roving horde. From my stool, he looked larger than life, a wizened mage about to impart his great advice. I would be a fool to question his wisdom.

"I was seventeen once," he said. "I used to think I was invincible. I know you want to go outside, see the sun, maybe even a zombie. You will one day. And you'll long for the comfort of this home. You'll wish to unsee the horrors of the world as I know it. But I'm still able to provide for us both. And I made a promise to your mom to keep you safe. I intend to keep it."

My shoulders slumped and my heart dropped. I couldn't argue with him. I saw the fatigue and grief he wore on his face every time he returned from the outside. I could tell the world was a living nightmare even though I never experienced it on my own. I only wished he would trust me as much as I trusted him.

"When I'm eighteen, then?" I asked, holding back tears.

He didn't promise or even say yes. He just gave a half-hearted nod and began to walk down the narrow hall to his room. Sadness had returned to his face, the guilty eyes I had grown accustomed to.

"Take your antidote," was all he said.

I obeyed and went to the icebox. The antidotes were in small vials and sat in a tray on the middle shelf. I had to take them every other day to ensure I didn't contract the airborne virus. I never minded taking it. It was orange and tart and sweet. Dad said he flavored it to hide the acrid medicinal taste. It was one of the many ways he convinced me he was a genius.

My father convinced me of many things. It didn't take much for me to believe him. My story is evidence that a parent can tell their child any number of lies about this world. After all, my world did only exist from my individual perspective. How could I have questioned it?

2. Hannah

I had no idea what I was going to do with my life.

It always seemed very arbitrary to me that a person had to start making decisions about their long-term career goals in high school. I had no idea what I wanted to do when I was sixteen. Eight years later, I still didn't know.

I went to community college in Los Angeles. I was majoring in linguistics. Before that, psychology, before that, communications, and before that, journalism. I was thinking about switching back to psychology. They knew me well at the student affairs offices. I was Hannah Moreno, the girl who'd likely be in school forever.

David had made this point to me on numerous occasions. He was my best friend since the seventh grade and I trusted him to administer tough love when I needed it.

"You just gotta finish it out and graduate," he told me. "Exit out into the real world, live a little bit of life, and if a life's passion suddenly -poof!- appears in front of you, maybe you'll go back to school for it. It's not a big deal."

That was, of course, easy for him to say. David was a computer whiz-kid since he learned how to read. He always knew what he wanted to do with his life. He graduated high school early, finished his four-year program, and already had a fairly well-paying job at a growing start-up.

He was sitting next to me at our usual lunch spot, a red plastic-coated picnic table in the center of my campus. It was a modest lunch. He chewed on an egg-salad sandwich while I picked at a bunch of grapes from a Tupperware. He was wearing his favorite plaid button-up and his thick black-rimmed glasses. His weird patchy beard was starting to grow back. I liked it better when he was clean-shaven.

He wasn't making any eye-contact with me as he talked. A trio of blonde women were tossing around football on the grass in sports bras and yoga pants. They were leggy and gazelle-like. David's attention was otherwise occupied.

I wasn't jealous. Sure, there were a few times in our friendship when I thought we might date or even end up together in the long run. David admitted to considering me on occasion as well. But we never liked each other at the same time, and that was okay.

"Remember Scott?" he asked me. "That kid with the bleach spot on the side of his head?"

I did not. David finally looked at me when I didn't respond.

"We used to climb into his window drunk and do experiments in his microwave?"

"Oh!" A fond memory of freshman year shenanigans popped into my brain. "The Peeps would get so blobby." David laughed, but I realized why he brought up Scott's name. He was a grade-a doofus and David was making an unfair comparison. "I am not like him!"

"Sure, you are. He switched majors three times sophomore year and took a leave of absence. Got a nowhere job for a bit, then headed back to school out east. He's a freshman again. He's twenty-five and a freshman- which would all be fine, except he still doesn't know what he wants to do."

He gestured with his sandwich as he talked. A clump of eggy mayo splatted on the ground.

"I'm twenty-four and a senior," I defended myself with an air of bravado. "A super senior."

"As a linguistics major. If you switch back over to psych, you're basically a second semester sophomore."

I pouted. He was right.

"I just always feel like I'm making the wrong choice," I said. "We get this one life to live and I don't want to fuck it up."

"You can't live like that," he said. "You can't guess the things you'll end up regretting. Consider my tattoos for a moment."

He rolled up his sleeves to show me the collection of tattoos on his forearms. He had an assortment of designs crawling up his arms, animals and tech gadgets, gothic lettering. I had seen him without his shirt on a number of occasions. The designs continued onto his chest and stomach and camouflaged behind the smattering of hair between his pecs he called his "taco meat."

"I'll admit to you here and now that I'm not in love with all of my tattoos. But I don't regret any of them. When I look at them, I remember the time in my life when I got them. I remember where I was and the people I was with. They're like a time capsule."

I stared deeply into the crossed-eyes of a blurry misshapen teddy bear on his wrist.

"Even that one?" I teased.

"Especially that one," he said.

He pulled his sleeves back down to cover artwork I knew I'd regret were it permanently on my body.

"Analogy noted," I said. "What about making the choice in the first place? How do I decide what to do with my life?"

"Really asking all the hard-hitting questions, aren't you Hannah?"

I shrugged. He chuckled and finished his sandwich. He wiped his fingers vigorously on a napkin.

"Okay," he said, finally giving me his full attention. My dark eyes reflected against his lenses. "This might sound a little silly coming from me as an atheist, but hear me out. I have found that people are passionate about the things that make them feel closer to God, or whatever their definition of God is. Nurses and care-givers want to heal, protect, and nurture. Artists want to create, provoke or influence thought. Some people just want to be rich, to have power, to be revered. But I don't think that's you. I think you want to understand the world around you and enact positive changes with the lessons you've learned. I think your empathy and humanity drives you - which is, in part, why you're terrible at making decisions."

I scowled at him. He really had to end with a burn, didn't he?

"Also," he added. "You need to figure out if you want your career and your passion to be the same thing. Just ask yourself, am I okay with monetizing what I truly care about? And am I able to be happy earning money doing something that means very little to me?"

I couldn't answer either of those questions.

His advice stuck with me after we parted ways and I walked back to my house. I lived in East Hollywood, which was neither the touristy Hollywood proper, nor the cute and trendy West Hollywood. My neighborhood was home to second generation El Salvadorians and an old Korean retirement home. It was a community of sweet families fighting against low incomes, astronomical rent, and gentrification. The sidewalks were broken and the gutters were filled with trash. The trunks of the dead trees that lined the streets were tagged with bad graffiti. But there was a woman who sold street-corn, bacon-wrapped hotdogs, and pupusas out of a rolling cart, so that was a perk.

I lived with my mom. She was short and skinny. Her black hair was teased and curled. She loved to wear hot pink lipstick and slingback wedges. We shared a ground floor two-story apartment. During the summer, the cockroaches always tried to crawl in under the front door. Half of the walls were glossy painted cinderblocks and the floor was covered in cheap terracotta tiles. It was definitely a space meant for either a single person or a couple, but we got by. I slept on the fold-out futon in the living room. I definitely was never allowed to have a boy sleep over. Not even David.

We moved after my parents' divorce. I was fifteen. My dad relocated to San Diego. My sister Daniella got married to a dentist and my brother Hector just sort of drifted off. He drove up north and fell out of contact with everyone. He didn't say goodbye.

I was the youngest, but in many ways I felt consummately stuck in the middle. Daniella was the first born, the golden child. Hector was the only boy, but also the fuck-up. And while I desperately tried to attain anything close to the perceived success of my sister, I worried that my nature was more like my brother's; wandering and helpless.

As I got older, I carried the guilt of the debt I accrued during my years of schooling. My mom worked two jobs to support me. I had a part-time job at the library, but my occasional minimum wage hardly made a dent in our bills.

We'd argue sometimes about silly pointless things. They were the sort of arguments that I imagine only occurred due to living in such a tiny space. Once, I broke a framed picture of my brother in a moment of anger. My mom didn't yell at me that time. She just stood in the back alleyway for a while, smoking a cigarette and watching the sunset while a neighbor's quinceañera music echoed from down the street.

In hindsight, the stress I carried in my life was trivial. I can look back upon my angst with dark amusement. I had a life and it wasn't terrible. It was tragically beautiful and depressingly simple. I had family. I had friends. I had a future. And despite my inability to make them, I had choices. In fact, I had the choice to be indecisive.

Then one day, all of that changed.

3. Lothryn

I was used to the pattern of my father leaving in the mornings. It was rare for him to stay inside with me, though it did happen on occasion.

I'd frequently find him in the bathroom standing in front of the mirror. He'd stare into his own pale eyes with grim dissatisfaction, as if his very existence were a disappointment. Then he'd turn on the faucet, wash his face, and rinse the loathing away. He'd never look at me in this way; I was the symbol of all he could achieve. I was his hope. I reminded him not to give up.

I'd watch him pack for the road with a long canvas duffel bag. He had a wondrous armory in his bedroom. There were axes, swords, pikes, and knives as well as crossbows, pistols, and rifles. He usually took the rifle and a machete. He told me he would teach me how to use the weapons effectively, but he never did.

It was the day after my seventeenth birthday and I had decided I would continue to push for him to take me along. I followed him after he locked his bedroom door and moved to the living room. He put a handful of granola bars into his cargo pocket.

"I've been exercising," I said to him.

He grabbed his dirty tennis shoes and smiled at me as he slipped them on.

"I can tell," he said. "You look stronger than I was even at your age. Make a muscle."

I flexed my bicep. A meager mound rose under the flesh of my arm. Dad squeezed it softly.

"Pretty good," he said proudly. He ignored my leading tone and went back to tying his laces.

"I mean, I should be able to carry more now."

"Lothryn, you're not coming."

I crouched down to his level. I needed him to know I was serious.

"You said yourself that your eyes are going. What if you miss finding another survivor?"

"There are no other survivors," said Dad. "At least not in this city. Don't you think I would have found one if there were?"

"But I heard a voice the other day," I said to him. His eyes locked to mine. Color drained from his face. I had his full attention.

"What sort of voice?"

The way he looked at me made me nervous, as if I had said something wrong.

"Well, it sounded like a woman," I said. "She wasn't screaming or wailing like the creatures you've described. She sounded happy. It was very far away, but I thought I heard laughing. It was sweet and melodic."

Dad closed his eyes and nodded. He sighed deeply and stood.

"Yes," he said. "I had meant to tell you about this. Those are the cries of sirens. That's what I call their breed of zombie. They are not women. Not living, at least."

Be brought his hand to my shoulder and massaged it with his thumb.

"How I wish I could give you a woman... someone to call your first love. But the world isn't fair. Pay no more attention to those friendly feminine voices. I told you, the zombies are evolving to draw us out. They won't be able to sustain themselves much longer. They will try to trick you, garner sympathy if they have to. It's when you let them close, that's when then they get you."

His grip on my shoulder tightened.

"So you what?" he asked. He loved to test me.

"Shoot them before they can even get near you," I said, rattling off his lessons like a trained parrot.

"Where?"

"The Brain."

"Or?"

"Decapitate them, or burn them," I muttered. "Chop them up into little pieces to make sure they're dead."

"That goes for anyone," he said with an air of melodrama. "Even me. Should I turn up dead or come home with a bite."

I rolled my eyes.

"You don't have to drill this into me every day."

"All this talk about you trying to come with me, it sure feels that way," he said.

He took his bag and started towards the door. He left me to feel the guilt of my behavior. How dare I question the man who tirelessly protected me?

"I'm sorry," I apologized.

"Take your antidote and lock the door," was all he said to me.

I followed his instructions. After the door shut, I set the door chain and the swing guard, locked the two deadbolts, and the knob lock. There was no question in my mind that my father was venturing forth to brave the danger of zombies in order to scavenge for our continued survival. But that wasn't the truth. That wasn't the world that existed outside of our doors.

My father exited our apartment instead into a rundown, yet livable courtyard with picnic tables and a functioning swimming pool. There were people living in other units, mostly starving artists who had moved to Los Angeles to pursue their impossible dreams. Just on the other side of the door I locked, were frequent notes left by our landlady.

She was an old Greek woman named Idola and she was not a fan of my dad. Maintenance workers and building inspectors alike had been thwarted by our bolstered security for over a decade. The addition of locks violated the terms of our lease. Secondly, our fourth-floor walk-up faced the street, so any curbside appeal was tarnished by our boarded-up and newspapered windows. And, of course, like many in the overpriced apartments across the city of Los Angeles, he struggled to pay rent on time.

Idola often waited for him in the lobby to complain about his delinquency in the mornings, but she never pushed him too hard. She was justifiably afraid of the wild-eyed man who had hermitted away in her building for years; the man who carried a bag that poorly concealed the shape of a rifle. She probably thought he was a hitman.

But he didn't do anything nearly as exciting. My father worked in a neighborhood convenience store for forty hours out of his week. He had a uniform, a green bowtie and a red vest. He sold prepackaged junk food and cases of alcohol to an endless stream of stoned Californians. And knowing my father, or at least his temperament, he hated every moment of it.

I never saw his uniform. He left it in his car. He exchanged it for his bag of weapons. He'd shed his cruel lie and adorn his miserable truth, the act of which reminded him daily that he was a loser. But this is a fact I can only assume and also hope for.

I, on the other hand, was left to my own devices for eight hours a day. I was an obedient child. Dad convinced me that being especially loud, attempting to go outside, or prying the boards and newspaper from the window to look at the outside world would bring zombies upon us. I was tempted, but I couldn't allow myself to live with that guilt.

Instead, I had my hobbies- hobbies that I could only assume were the standard practices of a teenage boy. As soon as I entered puberty, I discovered nearly in sync with the hair growing up my legs, that I was getting stronger. My dad taught me to do sit-ups and push-ups, jumping jacks and squats. I would play the cassette player he gave me. I only had two cassette tapes. One by Hughie Lewis and the other by The Ramones. I had to play them quietly, especially The Ramones. They sang in a language my father never taught me, but I knew all of the lyrics- just not what they meant.

There was an old clothing catalogue in our house as well. It was something I never cared about as a kid, but as soon as I turned twelve, I had become increasingly interested in the models within its pages. They wore skirts and dresses, exercise gear and swimsuits. And though Dad and I had a few open conversations about how the images made me feel, I became ashamed of how often I desired to gaze upon the catalogue women and of the things I did while gazing upon them.

I took up drawing as well. I used the models as inspiration, or as muses, my dad would say. My dad taught me to make charcoal and brought me a journal. In time, the sound-proofed walls of my room contained an additional layer of drawings, of people I'd never meet and a world that seemed so foreign, it couldn't have existed.

I did look through my window. It faced the alley. I had picked a small hole in the newspaper with my finger giving myself splinters as it squeezed between two wooden planks. Perhaps by design, my window faced the alley.

Once, I saw a dirty, disheveled man lumbering by the dumpster. He groaned and yelled to himself. He picked through the trash and threw glass bottles against the pavement. Dad never taught me about the rampant homelessness in American cities, nor did he teach me about the many manifestations of mental illness. I only knew of zombies, and thus, that's what I saw.

4. Hannah

The Student Affairs Office at my college was an old, dusty room with matted orange carpet and wilted beige curtains. My counselor sat at her desk in the corner. Her name was Lauren. She was a fashionable woman not much older than me. Her acrylic nails matched her pink blazer. I watched them clack away at her keyboard beyond an assortment of miniature plastic succulents.

Lauren had feigned delight upon seeing me as I sat down for my appointment. She forced a second smile as she looked up to address me.

"Hannah Moreno."

"Yes," I said. It was an odd thing to have to confirm my name. Lauren clearly remembered me.

She pulled up my file on her computer and frowned.

"You want to switch majors... again. To psychology... again."

I tried to ignore the judgement in her tone. Why did she care anyway?

"I do," I said. "I've always found psychology fascinating."

"Since when?" she challenged. "It says here that you only have one of the required credits."

"Since always," I insisted. "I don't think having multiple interests is by any means rare. And despite the lack of courses, I find I use psychology in my everyday life. In fact, just the other day, I used the word Oedipal... and not to describe food."

Lauren looked back to me with confusion. She didn't get my joke.

"You know, Oedipal... edible. They're near-homophones. Jokes are always more funny when you have to explain them, right?"

I chuckled awkwardly. Lauren only blinked at me. A fly was trapped in between the glass and the window screen.

"I see," she said.

I decided to make an appeal. Her resistance was something I hadn't anticipated. I had a hard enough time convincing myself to change majors. Lauren the student affairs counselor wasn't about to talk me out of it.

"I don't see a future in what I'm doing. I don't want my entire education to culminate in a piece of paper that means virtually nothing."

"I don't know if a major change to psychology will make you feel any more at ease," said Lauren. "I'm going to be real with you; employment opportunities in both of these fields are both sparse and competitive. It's a shit time in America to be a college graduate looking for work."

"Trust me, I'm well aware," I argued. "But as a career, becoming a psychologist seems a bit more tangible to me than becoming a linguist. It feels like majoring in communications."

"I majored in communications," replied Lauren.

I put my head in my hands. My second attempt at humor had failed. Worse, it had burned the woman I needed to convince.

"Please, just let me change. Doesn't the school want more of my money?"

Lauren sighed and started to type up the paperwork. I slumped back into my chair in relief.

"One of these days you're going to have to step outside these walls," she said to me.

I resisted rolling my eyes at the irony. The office was full of recent graduates like Lauren who had never actually ventured far beyond the walls of their alma mater. But then her words of dissent started to fester in my brain. Any certainty I had going in to the appointment seemed to drift away from me and out the open window where it took flight on the wind.

I decided to hang out with David that afternoon. We met at the subway station and walked to the convenience store to pick up snacks to accompany our video-game playing. It was a frequent stop for us. The store was cute and old-school. The employees had to wear green bowties and clashing red vests.

He told me a story about work and shook his head at me as I told him about my choice to change majors.

"So, important question," he said as we perused the snack aisle.

"Can we not talk about my decision to further imprison myself in schooling?" I interrupted him.

"Hey, I already said my piece. I was just going to ask you who your favorite off-brand cereal mascot is."

I stopped and looked at the array of oddly drawn cartoon characters on various pastel boxes of cereal. One of the many things I loved about David was his ability to distract my mind with delightful non-sequiturs.

"That is an important question," I said with a giggle. I picked out a box featuring an oddly angry-looking rabbit. "Definitely this one."

"Aw, no love for the unspecified blue dinosaur in the chef hat?" he replied with a laugh.

"David, that is clearly a stegosaurus crossed with a triceratops, a steggatops if you will. By the way, this conversation fucking reminds me- I kind of want to do shrooms again."

David cocked his head at me. He wasn't much for recreational drugs. He was more of a beer guy.

"Why?"

"Because I'm stressed out all the time for no reason and I want to go on a mental vacation," I said.

"Well, I'm pretty sure my friend- well my friend's friend, Benton still sells shit," David replied with an apathetic shrug.

"Benton? What kind of name is that?"

"I know. Benton Stuart," David specified. "He's got one of those names that sounds like it should be reversed." He finally decided on a box of blueberry Poptarts. "Anyway, he works at a weed dispensary, but he'll sell you anything else out of the back of his Prius in the alley behind the store."

I scrunched up my face.

"How sketchy. I don't know why shrooms aren't legal anyway. They grow out of the earth. Research suggests it could be medically beneficial to people with depression, OCD…"

"Crippling indecisiveness," David added pointedly. I was carrying two bags of chips. I still hadn't decided which flavor I wanted.

"It's not crippling," I muttered and forced myself to choose.

We set down our bounty in front of the cashier. I had seen him a lot. He looked to be in his fifties with his scraggly salt-and-pepper goatee. He was slender and tall with very pale blue, almost gray eyes. He had an intensity about him that always made me feel uncomfortable.

He rang up our items methodically. He asked if I had a club card as if he were reading it from a script.

"No," I said quietly. "I don't know if I want to be part of your club."

"I got one, Hannah" said David and he slapped the laminated card down on the scratched glass counter above the rows of colorful lottery tickets.

The man made nervous eye contact with me as we finished the transaction. It didn't feel lecherous or malevolent, but it made me uncomfortable nonetheless. Thankfully, David noticed as well.

"Hey, why are you staring at my friend?" David said, puffing out his chest.

"Oh sorry," said the cashier. "I just heard you say her name was Hannah. Is that with an H at the end?"

"Um, yes," I said nervously.

"That's a good name," he said. "A palindrome. My wife's name was a palindrome."

The explanation for his staring, though bizarre, was oddly comforting.

"Oh," I said. "What was her name?"

I expected to hear a name like Eve, Anna, or Elle.

"Solace," he said. Or that's what it sounded like. Then, he handed us our bag. I turned the name around in my head a few times, trying to make it spell the same way backwards and forwards. Solos, Sollos, Sullus, Sauluas, Salas, Sallas...

"Sallas," I said aloud to David later. I wrote it out for him on a piece of scratch paper.

"Hmm," he studied it briefly. "Sounds like a made-up name. That guy doesn't seem right in the head."

I couldn't help but agree.

5. Lothryn

Two days after my seventeenth birthday, my dad received the phone call he had been waiting for his entire life. He was sitting in his car after work, smoking a cigarette and watching the sun set. He was a writer and he spent his spare moments daydreaming about the stories in his mind that had never found a platform to be shared with the world.

He didn't have any friends or remaining family. There was no reason for his phone to ring except to be harassed by a collections agency. And yet, that evening when his cellphone rang from an unknown number, he answered.

There was a woman's voice on the other end, dark and cool. Her accent was European, English perhaps but hard to place. She asked for him by name.

"Who is this?" he asked.

"I represent Delphi House Publishing. I have in front of me one of your manuscripts."

His heart raced, he sat up immediately in his seat.

"Oh! Which um, manuscript, is it?" he said as if there were more than one he had ever completed.

"The novel," she replied. "Awakening: The Twilight of Eramice Odris."

It was a thrill just to hear the title on another person's lips. She had even pronounced it correctly.

"Of course, that one. I actually recently just changed the title, what with the success of that whole teenage vampire saga."

"We like the title and we like the book," she assured him. "I understand that it's part of a whole series."

"It is! I've written a lot more- I'm in process of, well not for a while, but I could-"

She cut him off.

"We'd love to see whatever you have. If you're available, we could meet with you in-house as soon as tomorrow. We have a one-thirty slot. Are you available?"

"Yes! I mean I have work, but fuck work!"

It was a side of my father I never got to see, the desperation, the yammering. My dad was consummately melancholy, the weight of his own post-apocalyptic world on his shoulders.

"I'll put you down for one-thirty," said the woman "Do you have a pen to take our address?"

He reached clumsily around in his back seat which was strewn with weapons for fighting zombies. He did not find a pen, but his forearm found the thick serrated spine of a hunting knife. It tore his flesh with its teeth and spilled his blood onto the upholstery. He cursed into the phone.

"Sorry, no," he grunted, trying to mask his pain. "No, I don't have a pen. Can you text it to this number, please?"

"No problem. See you tomorrow."

Then, she hung up and my dad celebrated, dancing in his car.

He wrapped his wound in a scrap of gray fabric he tore from a t-shirt. I imagine as he did, he considered what it would mean to find success in the selling of his book. How much change would have had to come to our lives for him to have told me the truth? Would we have moved out of the apartment? When would he have told me that the world wasn't the very hellscape he described? Would I have been able to forgive him for his lies?

He came home that night with an extra spring in his step. I noticed it immediately. Even the special knock at our door he did to let me know it was him had a nervous insistency. I noticed the bandage around his arm promptly after he entered.

"It's just a scratch," he insisted.

He reached into his backpack and pulled out a few vials of antidote. My entire life, he had always managed to scavenge more for me. He said there were vats full of the stuff at the old hospital; he just wasn't strong enough to carry the vat home. He also revealed a few bags of corn chips and some canned soup.

"Is that all?" I asked him. I tried not to show my disappointment.

He shook his head and grinned. He pulled out some batteries for my tape player and a new cassette. I couldn't believe how lucky I was; I would finally get to listen to new music. I studied the case, trying to read the strange characters that covered the plastic box.

I caught my dad staring at me as I investigated my treasure. He was smiling and yet sad. Tears welled in his eyes.

"What?" I asked.

"I just love you so much," he said.

"I love you too." My eyes darted to the bandaged wound on his arm and back to the grief in his eyes. "You didn't get bitten, did you?"

"No," he said, shaking his head with a chuckle.

"Don't scare me like that."

"Today was a very good day," he said. "And I think tomorrow may be even better."

These were words I had never heard him say before. The sentiment confused me. I couldn't even begin to fathom what he meant.

"I think we're coming to the end of an era and ushering the start of something new and wonderful," he added.

"Do you mean it'll be safe to go out soon?" I asked. "The zombies are dying?"

"Yes. That's what I mean," he said.

I embraced him. He squeezed me tightly. I held back my tears of joy.

"I'm going keep feeling it out, but change is in the air," he said. He held me away from him at an arm's length so he could look into my eyes. "When you go out in the world, please never forget how much I love you, how I took care of you all these years."

"How could I ever forget?"

I answered without even a moment's thought. My father was my hero. I couldn't imagine ever harboring any lasting resentment towards him.

"It may seem ridiculous now, but I imagine things will become very complicated."

I suggested that we listen to the new cassette together in celebration of his news, but he told me he needed some time to himself and that he had a big day of exploration ahead of him.

So we went to our separate rooms. I drew in my notepad while listening to my new cassette in headphones. It was different than my other cassettes. Dad said it was classical music, an opera called *Scipione* by George Frideric Handel. It was in a different language than the other two, but I could hardly tell the difference.

My father, meanwhile, was fishing his dusty old laptop out of its hiding place. He used it infrequently, but I'll always remember the sounds it made, the strange boops it exuded when it turned on and the clacking of its keyboard. I heard the sounds through my father's closed door, but he never told me what they were from.

The prospect of his meeting with Delphi House Publishing both delighted and terrified him. Mostly, he wanted to make certain his chapters were as polished and complete as they could possibly be. He hadn't worked on the story for years but it existed within his own complicated paracosm- a detailed imaginary world. The world contained his own language, the very same I had been raised to speak. He had a hand-written dictionary in a leather-bound journal on the shelf above his desk.

In many ways, my father was a creative genius misunderstood by the rest of the world. And like many of his kind that came before him, his frequent escapes into own his rich imagination came at the behest of any responsibilities of reality. He had neglected his health for some time. He was prone to blood clots and was prescribed blood thinners to prevent them- though he frequently forgot to renew his prescription.

And so, that night, on the eve of the meeting he thought would change his life, as he reached for the dictionary on his shelf, my father suffered a sudden brain aneurysm. He stumbled backwards and collapsed on his back in the center of his floor.

I didn't hear the thud. I was listening to opera.

6. Hannah

David had met a girl named Tara on a dating app. He showed me her picture. She was strikingly beautiful. She had wavy dark hair and a perfect body. She had a large tattoo of an apple tree on her back which made her look edgy. David was smitten.

They had a good first couple of dates and he wanted me to meet her. This was unusual. As close as we were, David tended to keep his relationships separate unless it was really serious. Oftentimes his partners were intimidated by his closeness to me. Girlfriends assumed I was secretly in love with him, while boyfriends were simply paranoid he would leave them for any woman.

"She says she wants to meet you," David told me. "She really likes me and wants to get to know my friends."

He was blushing and pacing around his apartment. He didn't know what to do with his hands.

"Chill," I said and patted the seat next to me.

"I can't chill," he explained. "I have no chill. It's been a while since anyone's made me feel this way."

He stood across from me with his hands awkwardly at his sides as if he were posing for his first day of kindergarten.

"And how does she make you feel?" I asked.

"I dunno. Like I'm important or like I'm an adult- a man. I think it's because she's so cool, like personality-wise. I feel like I've only dated anxious young lost people like myself. But she's a woman. And the fact that I can hold her interest at all makes me feel... great. Just great."

I tried to be happy for him, but his thesis statement on Tara's greatness left me more worried for him than anything. It sounded like he had put her on a pedestal after two days. He didn't have the complete picture of who she was. It sounded like he was on course to have his heart broken. But I didn't tell him this. I decided to reserve judgement at least until after I met her.

"Alright," I said. "Where and when?"

"I was hoping you would tell me that," he replied. "I need to take her somewhere trendy, classy, and maybe a little mysterious- but not gimmicky or tacky. You know me. I go to shithole dive bars. I have no idea."

"Now who's indecisive?" I challenged.

"It's not indecision if I don't know my options!"

We chose an intimate bar in Little Tokyo. It had a secret entrance through a narrow brick alleyway. Lights were strung above and space-heaters flickered with flames on the open patio. They had eighteen-dollar craft cocktails served in mason jars. Between the bartending staff's newsie wardrobe and faux-antique blue-collar furniture, I felt like I was on the set of an old Hollywood musical. We positioned ourselves at what was either a table or a large abandoned barrel.

"I'm going to get us some drinks," he said. "Tara likes an aviation. Have you ever had an aviation?"

"I have not. What's in it?"

"Absolutely no idea," he said. "There's a cherry in it. And lavender err... or maybe violet liquor. I don't know, but there's something bluish and flowery in it. It tastes like a lemony flower."

"I'll have whatever's cheapest, David."

Relief washed over his face. He looked handsome in his dark brown blazer. He was wearing a shirt with a floral print and his hair was slicked back.

"Thank you," he said and he maneuvered to the bar.

I was wearing a navy blue tank-top, jeans, and boots. I hardly had any make-up on. Yet I didn't feel underdressed until I saw Tara. She arrived in a form-fitting black dress and a red leather jacket. Her lips were painted and her lashes were curled. She looked like a movie star and commanded the attention of every set of eyes in the bar. She scanned the room like a lioness on the hunt. She smiled when she saw me and waved.

"Hannah?"

I waved back.

She half-ran in her high heels and reached towards me. It took me too long to realize that she expected to greet me with a hug. I leaned in and awkwardly patted her on her back.

"It's nice to meet you," I said. "Gosh, you're so pretty."

"Thanks," she responded with confidence I wished I had. She had likely heard it many times before.

"David's getting drinks at the bar."

She looked at him through the crowd without excitement, or at least the amount of excitement I would expect of someone in the beginning stages of a relationship. She turned back to me and shrugged.

"Good, we have time," she said. "I've already met David. Tonight's about meeting you."

She grinned coyly at me. And just like that, I decided I didn't like her. I wanted David to date someone who made him the priority. Meanwhile, Tara seemed like she enjoyed a game of cat and mouse. I forced myself to smile back at her.

"Are you from L.A?" I asked her.

"No," she said.

"Did you move out here to be an actress or a model?"

"No."

I quickly learned Tara giving one-word answers was par for the course. She was much more interested in learning about me. Any time I tried to steer the conversation towards her life or her interests, she'd flip the conversation so that I was the subject of the interview. I told her about the part of town I lived in, the classes I was taking, where I liked to hang out. It seemed like there was a checklist in her mind that she crossed off with every answer I gave her.

After too long, David returned with our beers and Tara's cocktail balanced uneasily in his hands.

"Whew, sorry about the wait," he said.

He brought his hand to Tara's waist and they kissed. It was brief and dispassionate. Tara left David wanting more.

"What have you been talking about?" he asked.

"Me," I said in a sort of sing-song tone that I hoped David would read into. He cocked his head at me. I began to chug my beer.

"Yeah, I've learned all about your bestie," said Tara. "You didn't tell me she was so interesting."

David must've been too blinded by his crush to hear the fakeness in her voice. He grinned from ear to ear.

"Aww, I knew you two would hit off."

"We sure did," said Tara. She picked the cherry out of her cocktail carefully and bit it from the stem. "That's good."

"Do you want another?" David asked her.

"No," she said. "I actually can't stay long at all. I have to wake up really early tomorrow for work."

"And where is it you work, Tara?" I probed.

"Just a boring office job," she said. "But my bosses are insane. They act like we're saving the world."

Moments later, she hugged David, kissed him on the cheek and departed. David returned to me with his shoulders slumped. He downed the rest of his beer and ran his hands through his hair.

"So you hate her," he said.

I wasn't sure if it was because he knew me so well or because I had been horrible at hiding it on my face.

"I do."

"Why? There's literally nothing wrong with her."

"Physically, sure," I said. "But she's a fucking weirdo! She grilled me with questions while telling me nothing about herself, she stayed for a total of thirty minutes, and she made you buy her an eighteen-dollar cherry." I gestured to the stem beneath the unconsumed aviation.

"She didn't make me buy her the cocktail. I assumed she would want one, so that's on me."

"She's imperious," I said to him.

"I don't know what that means!"

"It's like." I sighed as I struggled to come up with the definition. "It's like she acts like a queen and we're her peasants."

"That's a lot to get from her in only thirty minutes."

I never liked it when David was genuinely mad at me. It made my stomach tie up in knots. I think, deep down, I was terrified that he would abandon me, like my father, my sister, and my brother.

"Why are we fighting?" I asked him.

"Because I like her," he said. "And I don't think you gave her an honest chance. I think you hold anyone I could ever date to an impossible standard because you prefer us to both be single and miserable together."

That hurt. I shook my head at him.

"You're wrong."

I left David in the bar. We had driven there together, so I waited outside on the sidewalk for him to close his tab.

People were exiting Japanese restaurants beneath red and white paper lanterns. Down the street, a line was forming in front of a famous late-night ramen hotspot. Beyond the herd, I spotted Tara in her red leather jacket.

She stood on the corner as a shiny black car with tinted windows drove up beside her. It wasn't a ride share service; the vehicle itself didn't even have license plates.

As if she could feel my gaze, she looked back down the street at me and for a moment made eye-contact. She smirked with cruel amusement, folded her fingers into the shape of a gun and shot me with an imaginary bullet. As odd as it sounds, in that moment, I felt it pass through me like a ghostly premonition. A pedestrian obscured my vision. When he passed, Tara was gone and the black car was driving into the night.

7. Lothryn

I was surprised when my father didn't wake up and emerge from his room in the morning.

He had slept in a few times before, either due to sickness or a temporary depressive state, but these instances were rare. And never before had I heard absolute silence from the other side of his door. He snored when he slept, quite loudly, actually. It was a sound I had grown used to. I found it oddly comforting to know there was life in the house, sometimes vibrating through the walls.

I fixed myself a bowl of cereal and ate on the couch in the living room. I expected him to join me. He didn't. I cleaned my bowl in the sink and anticipated hearing his voice of gratitude interrupt my thoughts from behind. No voice came.

The sun was casting shorter lines of light through our boarded windows. The day was getting away from him. I decided to knock on his door; to wake him up, to ask if he was alright.

I knocked softly. No answer.

I knocked harder. Still, no answer.

"Dad?"

Maybe he had already left early in the morning, I tried to convince myself. But no, how could he have locked the chain locks?

"Dad- Are you going to get up today?"

My mind started to swim with the worst possibilities. Could something have crawled in through the window? My dad was too vigilant to be taken by surprise. Maybe he was wearing headphones as I so often was.

"Dad, I'm coming in."

I turned the knob and pushed open the door. But the door was stopped by a soft thump. I saw my father's bed, his orange afghan and tan sheets undisturbed. It was empty. On the floor, I saw my father's sprawled legs. His head was my doorstop.

My heart began to race. I pushed myself into his room. He was still and gray. His eyes were open and rolled back. I crouched over him.

"Dad. Dad. DAD!" I heard myself say.

I felt, in some ways, far away from myself. I looked to my dad's window. There was no sign of a break-in. No sign of struggle. I reached for his wrist to feel a pulse like he taught me. There was none. He was cold.

"Daddy?"

I felt like a lost child. Grief began to overtake me, but my own father's lessons echoed in my mind. He always warned of emotions clouding situations where practical action was required. I fought to control my breathing. If he was dead, I had to know why. Then, I remembered the bandaged wound on his forearm. How he had avoided its discussion the previous night.

I untied the torn cloth from his wound. The coincidence was cruel. The rough spine of a hunting knife had torn my father's flesh in a way that I, as a medically untrained seventeen-year-old, could only identify as the dental impression of a zombie. And because I had no context for the aneurysm that actually killed my father, I could only conclude that the zombie virus had claimed his life, and worse, that he would rise again as a cannibalistic shell.

Denial made room for anger. I couldn't believe that my father, who had instilled in me the rules for surviving an apocalypse, had broken one of his own commandments and not told his son about his infection and imminent death. He let himself die in our home where he would rise again and threaten my life. But I refused to let that happen. I didn't want to see him rise. I wanted to remember my father as I knew him. In some ways, I always will.

I leapt to the corner of the room where my father kept his weapons. There, shiny and completely unused, hanging on a hook was my father's medieval double-sided executioner's axe. He always said it was too cumbersome to wield against a moving enemy. But my father was motionless and not yet my enemy. He would never rise to become my enemy if I chopped off his head.

"Stop thinking," I told myself.

I took the axe in my hands. With every ounce of adrenaline in my system, it felt weightless, as if the weapon would float away from my fingers if it didn't hold it tightly enough.

I returned to my father and tried not to stare into his eyes. I knew he was dead, but there was something about his eyes, something pleading, something that made me want to sink to my knees and sob. I focused instead on his neck. That was the target I had to hit.

I positioned the blade so that it was hovering over his throat. If I struck well, one slice was all it would take.

"I love you," I said to him.

I raised the axe and struck with all my might. It took more than one swing. Three or four, I was distracted as blood speckled my face and pooled around my feet. When the head rolled free, I rushed into the hall. I fell to my hands and knees and puked out my cereal. And only then, because I knew I was safe, did I allow myself to cry.

I didn't often cry. In my seventeen years of an uncertain, worrisome, and mostly boring life, I didn't allow despair or solitude to be the causer of tears. Perhaps my father's penchant for vigilance quelled my need for natural emotional release. And yet, after decapitating his corpse, the only other human I knew to be living in the world, I was inconsolable. I didn't weep so much as I bellowed, moaned, and gasped. I punched holes in walls. I felt everything until, balled up in the corner of the kitchen at the end of a trail of broken china, I felt nothing.

Hours had passed. It could tell from the light it was late afternoon.

I only pulled myself to my feet with the realization that I needed to take an antidote. If my father's infected blood had entered my bloodstream, it was all I could do to stop my imminent death and transformation. There were twenty-three vials in the fridge; enough to last me a little over three weeks. I would have to go outside eventually to retrieve more from the location on my father's map.

But I was getting ahead of myself. The matter of most importance was the disposal of my father's corpse. The smell of its rot would not only be unpleasant to me, but would also risk drawing zombies with its scent.

I found a plastic bag beneath the kitchen sink, white and patterned with red smiley faces. I returned to my father's room, carefully lowered the bag over his severed head, and rolled it inside. It helped to focus on the mechanics of the task, rather than dwell on what I was actually doing. I tied the bag in a knot, carried the head into the kitchen, and placed it in the freezer next to a box of fruity popsicles. That was the easy part.

I took the body by the wrists and dragged it into the bathroom. It was stiff and unwieldy, but I got it into the bathtub and turned on the shower to help wash away the blood. Among my father's weapons, I found a bolt-cutter, a hacksaw, a machete, and a hatchet. They would be my chief tools.

From the afternoon to the deep of night, I snipped and sawed, I hacked and chopped. I reduced the body into small grisly morsels which I fed to the sewer system, via the toilet, one flush at a time. The limbs weren't too bad, but the torso was a visceral nightmare. I kept sane by listening to the soundtrack of my newly acquired music, concentrating on the performative emotions of opera singers rather than enduring the tortured reality of my own.

In the early hours of the morning, when the task was complete, I cleaned the blood from the floor, though there was no saving the carpet. I washed myself and returned to my bed. I didn't eat or drink enough during the day. I had a headache and I was shaking, curled up with my knees to my chest underneath my comforter. My thoughts were so cyclical and delirious, they bled seamlessly into my dreams.

I dreamt of the repulsive gore in repetitive waves that I would awaken from, sweating and nauseated, before my heart slowed and fatigue set in to drag me to another nightmare.

It was evening again when I rolled from my mattress. I desperately need to pee. I made a peanut butter and jelly sandwich and forced myself to eat it. I don't remember it tasting like anything. I took another antidote. I stood in the dark of the apartment without lighting any candles and lumbered into my father's bedroom.

Beneath the crusty surface, I could feel the moisture from his blood in the weave of the carpet. The room was a shrine to my dad, consecrated by his death.

In the still of the dark, a green blinking light emanating low beside my father's desk disturbed the quiet gloom. I wafted towards it like a moth to a flickering candle. I found the curious device on its side, a machine with a pair of plastic hinges, a grid of square buttons dotted with old-world symbols, and a rectangular screen that glowed to life as I picked it up and brought it to sit on my father's desk. It was what I understand now to be his laptop, opened to his word processor and his novel as he left it.

I could not read the words on the glowing page. The symbols of the language I was taught were different than the characters lumped together in the towering collection of paragraphs. My finger was resting on one of the buttons and a growing line of "H" began to cut one of the passages in half. I released my rogue finger with fear for what I might've done. But the screen remained relatively unchanged aside from the position of the small black vertical rectangle that pulsed with a somewhat judgmental persistence.

On the floor, beside where I had found the laptop, was a small leather-bound journal. Under the blue light of the laptop, I flipped through the pages and found words in my language organized in a vertical column on the left side of every page. The right side displayed its corresponding word in the other language. I understood it to be a dictionary, and yet without knowing the intended pronunciation of the foreign characters, I doubted my ability to study and learn much of anything.

I was overwhelmed and confused by these uncovered objects. In many ways, losing my father had set me adrift with maps I couldn't decipher and tools I only knew how to use in theory. I wished he had listened to me and showed me the world so I wouldn't have to discover it for myself. Without his guidance, I no longer felt ready for the world outside.

Distantly, I heard the whirring of a police car and the percussion of a helicopter, the automated remains of machines employed by humanity to fight off the zombie threat. Their noises corralled the undead. I closed the laptop and shrank into my bedroom. I was alone and unprepared, I told myself, but I was safe inside.

8. Hannah

Tara stopped texting David after the night I met her. I told him what happened, how she had finger-gunned me in an oddly threatening way before disappearing into an unmarked car. David thought I was being ridiculous. But I wasn't being ridiculous, I tried to tell him. Rather, the scenario was ridiculous and I was simply reporting it to him. He wouldn't hear it.

Instead, he dwelled on the apparent loss of their potential relationship. Though he would never admit it to me, I think David saw Tara as a trophy. She was society's idea of pinnacle attractiveness. He couldn't believe a woman so physically stunning would be into him. He lamented less the loss of Tara in particular and more the idea that he would never have the chance with a person as beautiful ever again. Perhaps I was selling David short.

"What did you even know about her?" I asked him.

We were at the neighborhood ice cream place. It was a favorite hangout spot for us. David had an unhealthy obsession with ice cream. It was one of those bougie spots with experimental flavors like lemon-curd matcha or rosemary pistachio-brittle. We usually got chocolate or vanilla. David licked chocolate from the rim of his cone, a defensive scowl taking over his face.

"What sort of question is that? I know a lot about her. I wanted to know more about her."

"What sort of things do you know about her?" I probed. "What are her hobbies?"

"She likes video games."

David must've seen the doubt in my eyes, because he followed up quickly.

"I said I liked video games, mostly RPGs and she said me too."

I tried not to laugh.

"That's not- She could have just been saying that," I said.

"A lot of girls like video games! It's not eclectic."

"I realize that," I said. "I'm one of them. And Tara could like video games too, but unless she went off in specific detail, she also could have just said 'me too' to make you feel like you have something in common. What else do you know about her? Does she have friends?"

"We didn't talk about her friends."

"What did you talk about?"

"Mostly about how handsome she thought I was."

Melted ice cream clung to his scraggly beard hair as he bit into the cone. I deeply sighed.

"What about her work?" I asked.

"Ah, that I know," said David proudly. "She works for Delphi House Publishing. I remember because I made a joke about the Oracle of Delphi and she said my intelligence is sexy."

I refrained from commenting on how easily I felt Tara's compliments manipulated him.

"She doesn't look like the sort of person who would work in publishing," I said instead.

"You know, for someone you derided as being a judgmental interrogator, you're certainly being that to Tara," he said. "Like the pot and the kettle, a very hot and innocent kettle who decided to ghost me."

"Creepy finger-gun," I replied simply. "I reserve my right to judge."

David rolled his eyes at me.

I found myself in the campus library later that day. I should have been working on schoolwork. It was, after all, what I was there to do in theory. But instead, I decided to follow up on the scant information David provided on Tara.

I found a website for Delphi House Publishing. It was modern and neatly designed. A large circular logo featured a dead black tree with a red snake in its branches. I clicked on a tab labeled "Who We Are." I found a list of employees there, rows of headshots and names beneath them. There were at least thirty of them, all beautiful women in their twenties with perfect hair and smiles. They dressed similarly. They projected the same energy. Among them, I found Assistant Publisher Tara Farris, grinning with the same practiced perfection as I had seen in person.

I searched for her on social media to no avail. In a way, that wasn't surprising. Tara Farris seemed like the sort of woman who would make sure you knew she deleted her social media profiles "because it's better for her spirit."

I returned to the website and clicked on her face. Her page was under construction. Every page aside from the home page and the employee page was under construction. Another person might have let their curiosity subside there, but there was something that rang false about the site. I felt almost as if I were being watched just for landing on the page.

I found the address for the company at the foot of the home page. It was close. Just a few blocks into Korea Town. I could walk there. And because I was clearly not getting any work done, I decided to.

It was late afternoon and the sky was turning gold. People were closing the gates on their nine-to-five businesses. Delphi House Publishing was supposedly in a strip mall between a hairdresser and a shoe repair shop. Not the glamorous location the site would have had me believe. But that wasn't too unusual for Los Angeles.

Sure enough, in a space that didn't look like it could hold more than an alleyway, I found a glass door featuring Delphi House Publishing's logo. While the door was glass, it appeared to have been painted black on the inside to keep passersby from looking in. The paint looked chipped, sun damaged, and old. I reached for a handle, but there was none to be found. If not for the hinges descending vertically along the left seam, it would have passed for a window.

The way to gain access appeared to have once been a keypad or card-reader, but that was ripped from the wall. Only snakelike wires emerging from a ragged hole remained.

"Excuse me, do you work there?" a woman asked me.

I jumped a bit and turned to find a stout woman with jet black hair streaked with cherry red. She had hot pink lipstick on her lips and teeth.

"Sorry to surprise you," she said. "My business is just next door. Did you move out?"

"Oh, I don't work here," I said.

"My mistake. You're pretty and young like some of the girls I saw here."

Like Tara, I thought as I politely thanked her for the compliment.

"Glad you don't work for them," she said. "Those people were up to some shit."

She lit a thin cigarette with a gold zippo and immediately coughed on the inhale.

"What sort of shit?" I asked her.

"Oh hell if I know. I just heard things, people moaning and screaming sometimes through the floor. They have a basement. I think they're of those weird Hollywood cults- you know, the ones that lure in actors as free acting classes, but then they take your money and brainwash you. They were here in force three days ago and now they're, poof, gone in the night. Even took their dumb fancy wall lock with 'em."

She kicked the bottom of the door with the toe of her gold-tipped flat and broke a hole in the glass. She gasped, the sudden unintentional vandalism coming as a surprise. But any guilt gave way for mischievous amusement.

"Fuck 'em," she cackled.

She let her laughter die, looking over her shoulder for anyone else who might've seen her indiscretion. Then she raised her eyebrows at me, flicked her cigarette into the parking lot, and trotted off to her run-down sedan.

I waited for the woman to drive away. Then I was alone in the strip mall. Or, at least I felt like I was enough to crouch down and look through the hole she created without feeling watched. I could see light inside emanating from a rectangular hole in the ground. The walls and floor in the narrow room looked stripped bare, any drywall or carpeting pulled away so that all that remained was dirty concrete.

I stuck my finger in the hole and tugged at the metal frame. With some force, the door clicked open. I stood as I pulled the door open.

What I did next would likely seem unfathomable to other more cautious people, but I always enjoyed touring abandoned buildings. I liked seeing an apartment cleaned, refurbished, and ready for the next tenant. I liked walking into construction sites where the work has been stalled or halted. I had once broken into a derelict mental health hospital with a group of delinquent friends as a teenager. The hairdresser told me the tenants of Delphi House Publishing had left. I took her word for it and I walked inside.

There was nothing else in the narrow hall other than the rectangular opening which, as I drew closer, I realized was a stairway to the basement. I half-crouched and peered into the lower level. The stairs were barren wood punctured with holes from torn-out carpet nails. I couldn't see anything but dirty cement below. I listened for signs of life before I descended the stairway, but I heard nothing. I didn't want any surprises.

What I found was a square, relatively large basement with cinderblock walls. A clear view of the space was partially obscured by the pinewood skeletal remains of the walls that once divided the room into smaller rooms. The wood was dotted with screws and dusted with the drywall that had been pulled forcefully from the anchors. It was draped in places with semi-opaque plastic sheeting. A few rolling dry-erase boards remained among the ruins.

I could see well due to four standing industrial work lights. They beamed harshly from the corners of the basement and cast a crisscross of shadows in the center of the room. I couldn't understand why they were left on; it was clearly no longer an active workplace.

Then, I heard a deep, wheezing cough.

I wasn't alone. My heart raced and my eyes darted in the direction of the sound. A lanky decrepit old man was shambling towards me. He looked filthy and deathly ill. Snot ran in rivers from his nose. His eyes were yellowed and bloodshot. His shirt was stained with blood and vomit. A thick wire rope scraped against the cement floor behind him.

"What are you doing?" He asked, delirious and gasping through phlegm for air. His teeth were gray. One fell from his mouth as he spoke.

"I- I'm sorry," I stammered. I bruised my shoulder backing into a vertical post.

"Stay away from me! Get out! Get out!" he bellowed.

And I did. I bolted up the stairs, stumbling in my panic, bashing my shin against the unfinished wood. When I escaped through the open door, I slammed it shut behind me, cracking more of the painted glass.

The man, whoever he was, wished to rot in peace, and I had every intention of granting that wish. I'm not sure what I expected to find at Delphi House Publishing, but each investigative step seemed to lead towards a deeper mystery than I was willing to uncover. As I showered and got into bed that night, I resolved to give up my casual investigation of Tara Farris. She ghosted David and was a blip in my boring life. I had my exciting brush with danger and I told myself that would be it.

9. Lothryn

Four days after the death of my father, I was awakened by the sound of a maintenance man banging on my door. Granted, I had no idea he was a maintenance man. I heard only the repetitive heavy knocks and yelling in a language I couldn't understand. I could only imagine that a roaming zombie had found the front door of the apartment, that he was somehow attracted by my scent or Dad's severed frozen head. As such, I bolted from my bed.

I found a pike in Dad's collection of polearms. My thought was that if the zombie persisted, I could unlock every lock except the chain lock, pull the door open and stab it through the small opening. A chill passed over me, giving me goosebumps. I felt vulnerable in only my underwear as I rounded the corner with pike in hand, but there was also a sense of excitement in the beating of my heart. I wanted to kill a zombie. I wanted to show the world I was ready.

But the knocking and yelling stopped before I even reached the door. I stood beside it, listening for movement, but I heard only the footsteps stomping distantly away.

My heart was still beating fiercely, but my shoulders sank at the lack of action. I was surprisingly disappointed, I realized, more so than I was relieved. I didn't just want to kill a zombie, I needed to kill one. I needed to know I could defeat one. I needed to see what I was up against.

It seemed likely to me that the zombie would return and when it did, I decided to allow it to enter my domain. I would hunt it from the shadows in the familiar comfort of my own home. I returned the pike to its place among the polearms and found a katana instead. It was attractive with a green-wrapped faux-ivory handle in a matching sheathe. It was tremendously sharp and not too cumbersome or weighty.

I buttoned up a flannel shirt and pulled on my blue jeans. By the time I was dressed, another heavy knocking resounded from my door. It was accompanied by yelling, but the voice was more insistent and higher pitched. It was the landlady, Idola, likely irritated that her maintenance man was ignored. Again, I had no way of knowing this. And so, as she endeavored to scold her least favorite tenant, I was eager to slay my first monster.

I positioned myself in a corner, beside the door where I could reach the locks and hide in the darkness as my prey entered. To my surprise, as I stood there, I heard the jingling of keys. I watched with astonishing horror as the lock on the deadbolt spun and clicked to its unlocked position seemingly on its own. Yet the other locks held and the banging and yelling commenced.

My heart began to beat intensely again and I had to remind myself to breathe deeply. I needed to remain focused and vigilant. I reached for the locks and unlocked them quickly before returning to my position.

Nothing. No zombie rushed chaotically into the space. The noise had stopped and all was silent. I trembled in my stillness, the katana drawn and powerful in my hands. Then, I watched the doorknob turn.

A near blinding light flooded into the apartment, calling attention to the dusty worn furniture, the sound-dampening blankets, and the boarded-up windows that had lent a sense of reality to my world for seventeen years. Poor Idola, she really had no idea she was about to enter another world.

She was old, older than my father. She walked with a bit of a limp in her flowy patterned blue dress. She looked fatigued and dazed as she took a hesitant step into the apartment. She stopped again to adjust her eyes and to scan the room. Her behavior seemed to align with what my father told me of the zombies, that they were often slow and shambling, that they behaved as if they were lost until they whiffed the scent of blood.

She seemed to notice something that caught her eye. In the living room, my father had a map of the city. He had circled locations perfect for scavenging or labeled those overrun with zombies. She walked slowly towards it, muttering something in a voice that was surprisingly clear, not wheezing as my father put it. But I felt I didn't have the luxury of studying her. If the zombie spotted me, she could kill me.

I ran at her. Idola turned to me, her blue eyes catching the light as they grew with terror. I stabbed through the chest and pushed her against the wall. She screamed horrifically, her throat gurgling with blood. For fear of her summoning more undead, I pulled out the katana. She fell to her hands and knees and I brought the katana down on the back of her neck.

Unlike the axe, it sliced through cleanly. Idola's head rolled away from her body as blood pooled around my bare feet. But the katana's blade broke from its hilt, clattered up at me, and cut a nick in the bridge of my nose, dangerously close to my eye.

I panted there for a moment, with my hands on my knees, gasping for air and reveling in the success of my hunt. Though a part of me was awash with nausea. Even if she were a zombie, it still felt like killing a human. Luckily, I did not yet know the truth.

The warm sunlight and the distant chattering of a bluebird reminded me that the door was still ajar. It was quiet in the apartment complex. I smelled the fresh air, I saw the wind pass through the palm trees. Somewhere far off, a loud vehicle's engine growled. I closed the door.

Idola's head joined my father's in the freezer in a black plastic bag. I took her body to the bathtub and began my process of dismemberment anew. It was less troubling for me than it was with my father in many ways. Her bones were thinner and crushed up easier into flushable pieces, though her pelvis gave me some trouble. Her body looked different from the women I saw in magazines. I was grateful for this. It was easier to think of her as a creature that had never been alive in the first place.

I took breaks intermittently, but in two days, the job was done. All parts of Idola, barring her head, had been flushed away into the sewers.

My success in killing Idola left me overconfident in my ability to slay all zombies. She hadn't put up much of a fight. She didn't try to bite or scratch me. And so, after an additional day of rest, I decided to exit the apartment for the very first time in my life.

I packed a bag with snacks, antidote, and bandages. I bound my father's machete in cloth and attached it to a belt so I could strap it to my back. In my waistband, I tucked a pair of sais. Dad told me they were great defensive weapons once used by warriors in Asia. Mostly I noticed how heavy and sturdy they were. They would bludgeon quite effectively. Finally, I armed myself with Dad's pistol. He had taught me how to load it, but I never had the opportunity to fire it. He told me to use it sparingly, for it was loud and could attract unwanted attention.

I pulled the map from the corkboard and folded it neatly into the pocket of my cargo pants. The old paper cracked at its seams. I decided that in the future I would need to draw another map.

In moments passed, I found myself looking in the bathroom mirror, the way my father always had before he exited into the world. I looked older, somehow, like I had aged a year every day since my father died. I had bags under my eyes and new wrinkles on my forehead.

"But I am ready," I said to myself. "You're all you have."

I ran cold water over my hands and splashed it over my face. I saw myself, a survivor, a killer, not a man to be fucked with.

Before I could overthink it, before I could convince myself to take it easy another day, I unlocked my door, stepped into the warm sun, and into the unknown.

10. Hannah

I was abducted on a Saturday afternoon.

I remember waking up that morning, the sun shining on my face through the blinds and the sound of Marisol selling her pupusas outside. I didn't roll out of bed immediately. Instead, I dicked around on my phone. I read a think-piece about social justice and watched a make-up tutorial for a look I would never attempt on myself.

I checked my messages. Still, no response from David. It had been two days since I told him about my adventure at Delphi House Publishing. I had texted him paragraphs. He didn't respond. It was unlike him to give me the silent treatment, but I could imagine my actions had annoyed him. I investigated a woman he was interested in without consulting him. But I would have thought the bizarre details I uncovered would have at least garnered an inquisitive response. His silence was both irritating and depressing.

My mom walked downstairs and began to cook some eggs. Her hair was in curlers which always made her look a bit silly. My favorite was the long one that rolled up her bangs like a bootleg Bettie Page. She hummed to herself as she often did, lending a melody to the percussion of the crackling eggs.

"Do you have schoolwork to do today?" she asked me.

"Always," I replied. "It's a cruel unending parade."

"So it would seem," she said pointedly.

She served up a plate of eggs with a side of salsa and toast for me. I sat up to eat it at the coffee table. She kicked back in her usual wicker chair with a plate of her own.

"I wonder how long you will be in school sometimes," she said to me. "I don't like the thought of how much debt you're racking up."

It wasn't the sort of conversation I liked with my breakfast. It was too taxing, too real. My mother was always oblivious when it came up to bringing up sensitive topics.

"You sound like David," I said.

"He's a smart boy. Very smart." She swallowed her eggs. "You should listen to him. How is he?"

"Fine," I lied.

"I talked to Daniella last night. She thinks you and David are in love and just don't know it."

That was exactly the sort of off-base intuition I expected from my sister who never spoke to me. I tried to not let her words upset me.

"Well, she's wrong," I said politely.

"How do you know?" My mother pressed me.

"Because only I know how I feel and Daniella's just pretending like she knows me to make her seem less shitty," I said less politely.

We ate in silence after that. Unfortunately, those were the last words I spoke to her. She was upstairs when I got dressed and left the apartment. I should have said goodbye.

David had given me the number of Benton Stuart, the guy who sold shrooms out of the back of his car. I texted him and he offered me an eighth for thirty bucks. I had no idea if it was a good deal or not, but I said, "cool" and hoped he didn't think I was naïve.

He told me to meet him in the alleyway behind his girlfriend's apartment complex. It was an easy walk up Vermont Avenue beyond the overpriced vintage shops. It was a beautiful California morning with cotton ball clouds in a brilliant blue sky. Warm with a cool breeze, just how I liked it.

I found Benton leaning against the back of his car. He was tanned and surfer-ish in a backwards cap and a white tank top. He was smoking a joint and talking on his cell phone. He hung up and casually waved me over.

"Yo lady, what's good?"

He gave me a brief hug, which surprised me. I wasn't ever so free with my body that I offered a hug to people I just met.

"Stuff," I blurted. "Stuff is good... I guess."

"Tite tite," he said. His eyes scanned my body from the ground up, assessing my nervous stance and hunched shoulders. "Girl, you need to relax."

"I know," I pathetically exhaled. "That's why I'm buying shrooms from you."

He cringed and scanned the alley for passersby.

"I mean, you don't have to yell it."

"Sorry."

I handed him my thirty dollars, folded as if I were going to discreetly tip a valet. Benton played along with me and slipped it into the back pocket of his shorts before handing me a little baggy of withered mushrooms.

"You done 'em before?" he asked me.

I nodded.

"So you know there's no way of knowing how high they'll get you. Mother Earth grows 'em all differently."

I'd forgotten that, though it seemed like a convenient excuse if he were lying and actually selling me dried shitakes.

"Thanks," I said.

"Hey, you used to do Tai Chi in Griffith Park with the college class, didn't you?"

I did. It was in my first semester, years prior. I was surprised Benton recognized me. I didn't consider myself to be especially recognizable.

"I was in the class too," he clarified. "I kept up with it. I find that it calms my nerves more than weed or shrooms ever can."

I cocked my head at what I assumed was the softer side of Benton Stuart.

"Wait, you sell me your shit and then you pitch me drug-free ways of coping with anxiety?" I challenged him.

Benton shrugged at me. His eyes darted again to the opening of the alleyway. He scowled.

"Oh no, we got a tweeker."

I followed his gaze to a confused-looking boy. He wore old, dingy clothes. He was pale, with dark hair and light eyes. He carried a bookbag on his back and a long blade wrapped in cloth. I noticed, far too slowly that he was also carrying a pistol. I felt my heart surge suddenly with adrenaline.

"Hey buddy-" Benton started to say. But then he was gone, a bullet passed through his forehead in front of my eyes. The shot rang out deafeningly. The echoes drowned out the world as sound tried to return to my ears in a single sharp-ringing note.

I couldn't breathe or think or move. Benton was on the ground and the boy was right in front of me. His arm was coiled back before the pistol-whipped me in the side of my skull.

I saw stars. I saw concrete. I saw black.

11. Lothryn

Dad described the outside world as a terrible place. The broken streets were littered with the debris of a fallen civilization where the skeletal corpses of fleeing humans were picked at by zombies, wild dogs, and vultures. The buildings were crumbling, overtaken by fire or smothered in snaking overgrowth. The sky was yellow and poisoned, columns of black smoke pulsed like sickly veins. Our home was a lonely citadel, untouched by these horrors. Yet the moment I stepped outside, I found his descriptions inaccurate.

My fourth-floor apartment opened into a courtyard with several closed doors that looked rather identical to mine. The sky, clouded and blue, was dotted with softly whispering palm trees. The air smelled relatively pleasant. There was some debris on the walkway, leaves, dirt, a scrap of paper, but it looked mostly tidy.

I stepped forward and looked down to the ground level. Inside a turquoise gate, a beautiful rectangular pool of water glistened invitingly. A large inflatable unicorn floated on the surface.

Perhaps if a family was playing poolside, I would have begun to question my reality. But it was deathly quiet that morning. I reasoned that my father's descriptions must have extended outside of the apartment complex. I wondered if he had spent some of his time outside cleaning up the other units. Maybe it was all to be a wonderful surprise for me one day. My mind seemed to have little trouble rationalizing the lies. The awful truth was too far outside the realm of possibility.

The sun poked up over the clouds and kissed my skin with its warmth. I closed my eyes. The warmth seemed to seep in through my pores and melt the encasing ice from my bones. I could have spent the day basking in the pleasant sensation, but Dad's tenants of responsibility and vigilance shook me from my comfort.

A stairwell was to my right, dark and gray in the shade of the eaves. I could almost hear my father's voice in my ears. "Always watch the stairs," he warned. If he had only watched the stairs, my mother would still be alive. A shiver ran up my spine. I drew my gun and proceeded into the stairwell.

I descended the three flights with extra caution. Every bird that chirped, every car that honked made me stop, listen, and reassess. At last, when I reached the ground level, I saw the further lack of disarray that proved antithetical to my father's description. A small brass fountain that depicted two children beneath a large umbrella trickled water into a well-maintained pond. A front lobby with a blue metal gate looked out into an orderly street. The apartment's mailboxes were clean and polished. Further, the cheap paper labels that adorned them showed no signs of the yellow of age.

Still, my brain rationalized. An apocalypse had ended the world- the rampant destruction was assuredly just out of view.

I backed away from the front gate and chose instead to depart through the side door beside the pool. I was struck by the water's clarity. A toy green army man had sunk to the bottom. I saw my reflection, a terrified boy holding his father's gun, distorted by the rippling surface.

The side door led to a narrow alley with tall yellow cement blocks obscured by garbage cans, broken washing machines, and graffiti. I nearly sighed in relief at the sight- finally, a visual that matched my father's words, never mind the newness of the graffiti and even the trash in the barrels. Through a crack in the wall, I found an abandoned overgrown lot with shanty homes, overturned shopping carts, and rusting heaps of garbage. But I didn't spot any zombies, no roving ghouls like I had seen peering through the gaps in my boarded-up window.

The alley ended with two large dumpsters at the end of a wider drive. I backed into this new space, worried suddenly that I might have been stalked by an unseen predator. But that proved to be foolish. I heard first the sound of a voice, deep and masculine, stringing together words I could not know. The hairs raised on the back of my neck with the understanding that I wasn't alone. I ventured too far. I wasn't careful enough. I could be overwhelmed.

I realized just how terrified I was to be killed by a zombie, to be torn apart screaming as my father had described to me. I considered my father, who had survived for seventeen years in a hellscape. How pathetic I would be to die in his very first battle in the open world.

I spun around on my heel with my finger trembling against the trigger of my gun. There were two of them, a male and a female standing beside a vehicle.

I didn't think. I didn't try to investigate. I only shot. The bullet found its mark between the male's eyes. The female clutched her hands to her ears. I closed the distance quickly and struck her with the butt of my gun.

She went still. She didn't bounce back up or hiss or claw. I searched my surroundings to see if the gunshot attracted other zombies. So far so good. Dark red blood was running out of the back of the male's head into a cracked section of pavement. Aside from the bullet hole in his face, he was in good condition. He looked young and healthy. The girl, too. In fact, I was struck by the curl in the corner of her lips, the curve at her waist, her soft skin- she was beautiful.

I didn't exit my house that day with the plan of taking anything home, much less what I could only imagine to be a monstrous killer. But the young woman, the siren, she was entrancing. I considered how little I felt I knew about the zombies, how different they were from my expectations. My father had shackles among his weapons- the very ones he had used to hold my mother before putting her out of her misery. I figured I could use them to hold my zombie. I could study her in the safety of my home.

I grabbed her by her ankles. She was light. Her skin was taut and warm like mine. I thought I could feel blood pulsing in her veins, or was it the beating of my heart in the tips of my thumbs. She was wearing lace-up shoes, jean shorts and a striped t-shirt. As I began to drag her across the asphalt, her shirt rode up exposing her navel and the beginnings of a tan brassiere patterned with little white llamas.

I nearly laughed. Whoever the girl was in life, I would have probably liked her personality. I certainly would have been attracted to her. I almost felt bad that I had bruised her face when I stuck her.

Dragging her wasn't working. I decided to change tactics and lift her over my shoulder. She smelled like cinnamon. It was admittedly risky. If she awakened, she could have bitten my back. So I moved quickly through the back alley. I pulled open the side door and raced up the stairs. My adrenaline aided me. She was light, but felt increasingly heavy as I took her up the stairs.

I plopped her in front of my door, panting and sweaty from the exertion. I dragged her the rest of the way, over hardwood and the carpet of my room. There was a metal support beam that floated in front of the south wall. It was a perfect place to restrain her. I found the heavy shackles with four manacles for wrists and ankles. They were a bit tangled, but I figured they would hold my prisoner tighter, so it worked out alright. My only worry was that she might chew through her limbs to free herself.

After I secured her restraints, I stood from a distance in the doorways. Sunlight was painting her in stripes of gold through the boarded window. She looked angelic, like some of the paintings Dad showed me in magazines. It was so hard to believe that something so lovely could be bad.

I wondered with a sudden hopefulness if she was actually a survivor. If she was being preyed upon by a zombie and I had come along and saved her. I might have been her hero. I had struck her, but it was misunderstanding that she would forgive- and I would forgive myself because, against all odds, we had found each other in our awful lonely broken world. It was naïve, I knew, but I couldn't help but wish for it.

I would know my wish was granted if she awakened and spoke to me in gratitude in the language that I knew. Any other language was that of the old-world savages, no matter how structured it seemed. If she screamed and hissed and growled unintelligibly at me, she was a monster. She would be merely a test subject that I would eventually have to put down.

12. Hannah

I dreamt of colors, of red and cream and silver and black stirred together, pouring onto surfaces and dripping from the edge. I dreamt of gore, of blood, bone, and viscera. The images faded behind a muddy gray-brown fog before a memory arose from a deeper well.

I was seven. It was Christmas Eve. My tummy was full on ensalada and tamales. Our tío was staying with us that year. He was my father's brother. He was skinny and sick-looking, missing some teeth and spotted with sores. Mom told us he was going through a rough time. I didn't know "a rough time" meant coming off meth. He had too much wine that night and started talking, well, ranting to me, my brother, and sister. He subscribed to many conspiracy theories, secret societies, ancient aliens - the sorts of things we neither knew nor cared about. I just remember being frightened by the intensity in his voice, the spit that flew from his scabby lips before my father pulled him away.

He died from an overdose years later. I never saw him, but in my dreams he was strewn on the floor of a dirty bathroom, his body writhing to its final stillness on a checkerboard of sweaty tiles.

My mind flashed through the faces of the rest of my family: my mother smoking in the alleyway behind our home, lines of grief upon her face, my sister seated in a chair beside a window, her head in her hands, my brother beside his van in empty field, blood speckling his skin, David in a disheveled apartment, confusion in his eyes and a shadow drifting closely at his back.

The visions blurred into darkness as the percussion of my throbbing head stirred me from my slumber. Why was I sleeping? At first I couldn't remember. My ears were ringing, a reminder of the gunshot that thundered inches from my right ear. Benton wasn't really shot in the face, was he? That was just another visceral nightmare.

I felt crusty, matted carpet beneath my legs. There was a smell of dust and stagnancy, the nostalgic displeasing funk of a cluttered thrift store. I could see the dust, wafting in air, illuminated by thin rays of sunlight. There was a window. It was obscured by wooden planks and yellowed newsprint. And it was quiet. The walls were muffled with foam mattress pads and quilts in shades of burnt orange and olive green. There were drawings of an amateur artist pinned proudly to the fabric.

At first, my understanding of my surroundings were too dreamlike to grip me with authentic fear. Then, I felt the weight of the shackles around my wrists and ankles. A shard of metal reflected light into my eyes. And there was the boy who had struck me, who had murdered Benton and dragged me to his lair. His icy eyes seemed to glow through the darkness. There was a machete in his hand and he stood in the open doorway with the twisted posture I would expect from a TV serial killer.

I screamed.

It was an unusual sound to come from me. I wasn't much of a screamer. I didn't shriek with surprise or delight as my sister often did. My response generally ranged from a delayed "Oh shit," to laughing out of discomfort. But there I was, screaming in the face of unknown horror.

He pounced upon me and I kicked back at him. I felt wet blood on my legs before feeling the pain of my shins bouncing against his blade. Words returned to my throat and I yelled for help while cursing at my captor.

I pulled like hell against my constraints without any regard for my wrists and ankles. The heavy steel bruised and tore into my flesh. Whatever he wanted from me, I was resolved to make him fight for it.

He tossed the machete aside and sat on my legs to still them. Then he yelled back at me in a language I had never heard before. It sounded Slavic. I couldn't place it. He meant to intimidate me, yet there was also panic in his voice. Either I was fighting too hard, or I wasn't the victim he imagined me to be. No, I decided, he was worried about how much noise I was making. He didn't want anyone coming to my rescue. That only made me scream louder.

He pushed off of me and pulled a gun, a pistol mere feet from my face.

My voice cracked to a whimper.

I remembered the fatal end of Benton Stuart and the bullet that passed through his skull. The memory of the gunshot echoed on repeat. Anxiety was overtaking my whole being. I could hardly think. He wasn't just going to kill me, was he? He had taken me for a reason. But maybe if I was too loud, he would decide I wasn't worth the trouble. Maybe he had already decided that. Maybe he was about to pull the trigger.

He said something to himself, more words I couldn't understand. Was it Danish? I couldn't place it. He looked scared. Sweat dripped from his dark hair and collected on his upper lip.

He pulled a roll of duct tape from the windowsill. I watched his finger sit on the trigger; trembling with unsettling indecision. I stared into the black barrel. And I was frozen as he wrapped tape around my mouth, sticking it tightly to my lips and hair. He wrapped my legs as well, carelessly bandaging my bloodied calves together to limit my mobility.

I listened to his words as he worked, as if in doing so I could somehow piece together a reason for what he'd done or for why I was there.

"Goer liebyister von und umehai," he said, still shaking his gun at me. "Hash lo go hat von cunar? Sarityn- pram hine go stauka."

I had spent a lot of time studying language. One might say too much time. I knew how to identify most languages as I heard them. It sounded in parts Russian, German, and Japanese. There was no consistency to it.

"Eya, sarit," he continued. "Tet hat ume gryna hashvon go, tet pallynas. Felet erer krow wi pallyn tet. Qitan hatsun go von, ume hine go koranos."

He looked at me expectantly, and I stared back at him, more lost than I ever had been in my life. What did he want from me?

"Qitan tet!"

I jumped. It was the loudest he had yelled. His face was red and the tendons strained in his neck. I thought then and there that he would pull the trigger. I imagined the tragedy of my death being a brief story on the evening news. I imagined my mother having to identify my body. Or worse, never being found at all. A tidal wave of anxiety and panic washed over me and I struggled to breathe as I uncontrollably sobbed.

The boy only stared at me, his head cocked to one side like an intrigued puppy. It was like he was an alien studying human emotion for the first time. I'm not sure how long he stood there, but after a while, he lowered his gun, retrieved his machete, and left me alone.

13. Lothryn

Dad told me that the zombies were once human. The humans died from an illness that made them reanimate after death. Their brains functioned only in the most primitive sense, clinging only to violent impulses and a desire to feed. They decayed just like corpses. Some shambled on for years with their bleached white bones barely held together by crackling sinew.

None of these descriptions matched the female I had chained to the support beam in my bedroom. I wondered if this was because of the change my father spoke of. Perhaps the disease was no more, or those infected had been cured.

She groaned in her sleep, not the groan of a monster, but in soft pained murmurs. I reached for my machete as my captive began to stir.

Her dark eyes fluttered open, finding first the beams of sunlight. I watched her think, struggling to understand her surroundings. Then, all too suddenly she saw me and her expression twisted into fear.

She screamed, just as my father told me she would. He explained the zombies that wore the faces of beautiful women were sirens. Sirens were an adaptive variant of zombies designed to lure men to their deaths. Their songs were sweet and their screams were horrific. Their screams had the power to summon a horde.

I was terrified of her bringing a legion of undead to overwhelm me, so I leapt at her. She kicked back at me wildly at me and my machete. She seemed to not feel the cuts that formed on her shins when flesh met blade. I found this disappointing, as it was the first evidence that aligned with my father's descriptions of zombies. They couldn't feel pain.

I tossed the machete aside, gripped her by her ankles and sat on them, anything to keep her still.

"Stop making noise," I hissed. "Damn it, hold still!"

But my words had no effect on her. She looked back at me with a complete lack of comprehension before screaming and struggling more. But there was one thing I knew she would understand; the threat of the pistol I'd shoved into the back of my pants.

I rolled off of her, stood, and pointed the gun at her face. Her screams silenced immediately. Her face returned to one of angelic innocence. She projected a face that had evolved to illicit guilt, or at least that's what Dad would've had me believe.

"You understand this, don't you?" I said to her. "My father taught you to fear this."

She stared into the gun. Dad said that zombie brains could still identify an object that had the power to kill them when they saw it; much like an ant knew to run from a finger that was about to crush it.

I reached for a roll of duct tape. Dad had always kept several in his closet. Once, I watched him use it to wrap the end of a baseball bat and ornament it with nails. He said he looked forward to testing it against a zombie's head, but I never saw any evidence that he ever did. As I kept the gun pointed at the siren, she resisted very little as I wrapped it around her head to cover her mouth and her ankles to prevent her legs from flailing.

In such intimate proximity, I couldn't help but notice how nice she smelled, like soap and flowers.

"You abominations are so convincing," I said to her. "Why did you have to be so beautiful?"

I wasn't sure why it made me so mad. I suppose I wished her to be the horrifying monster I was promised; that would have made things easier. I didn't like feeling like I was the bad guy. I made sure she saw my intent as I pointed the gun at her. I wanted her to know that I was powerful.

"Well, siren. I lost my dad because of your kind. He was my teacher. So now it's your job to teach me. Show me what you are, rather than what you pretend to be."

But she did little more than cower. I might as well have been talking to the wall.

"Show me!"

She flinched and began to sob. With her mouth sealed shut, her cries sounded muffled and far away like some wandering ghost.

It would have been easy to empathize with her, but I convinced myself to shut off my heart and treat her as a subject. So, I stood and marveled at her. I theorized how her brain might've functioned. She had clearly screamed in the old world language. I wondered if she knew what she was saying or if it was only an echo of the girl who once lived.

I remembered the handwritten dictionary in my father's room. It made sense to me that if I could speak the correct word in the other language, I could test her ability to understand.

I picked up my machete and went to my dad's room. Her sobbing followed me out, becoming louder as I left.

I pulled the dictionary from the shelf and thought of what I would say to the siren if I even could. "Do you understand?" came to mind. But I wanted to project a sense of civility and politeness as well. "Please tell me that you understand," I decided. I found the word, "please" easily enough written beside characters I had no ability to pronounce. It occurred to me that the dictionary was written in reverse for someone who spoke the old world language. But could a zombie read? Would a zombie read?

My thoughts were interrupted by music I had never heard before. It was a twinkly melody interrupted by an arrhythmic buzzing. It wasn't my cassette player. Whatever it was, the siren's sobbing had stopped.

I bolted back into my bedroom where I found the siren squirming. The song was emanating from some part of her body. I sat on her legs again and lightly patted her body. After her shoulders, my hands quickly found her breasts. They were soft and warm. I felt an odd leap in my heart when I touched them and I quickly pulled my hands away.

I discovered a hard rectangular shape in the pocket of her shorts. What I removed was unlike anything I had ever seen. The only thing I could equate it to was the laptop in my father's room. It featured the same glowing screen, only this displayed the face of a smiling bearded man. Then, the face disappeared and became a blue field cluttered with a grid of colorful symbols. The screen went black. I touched it and the screen returned. It was simultaneously mysterious and delightful.

I reached into the siren's other pocket and found a ring of keys, a tube of chapstick, and a collection of plastic cards bound by a black elastic band. They were embossed with digits and covered in swishy, colorful graphics. One had the picture of the siren on it. It wasn't a very flattering picture. She was much prettier in person.

The chapstick smelled very similar to the vanilla scented candles that Dad sometimes scavenged. They always helped diminished the musty smell. The key ring featured eight keys, some printed with adorable designs with the paint chipping away. They were accompanied by a square plastic keychain with a picture of a sunset behind a swirling mixture of glitter and water.

I found the objects unusual and sad. They were artifacts of whoever the woman once was, of no use to a scavenging flesh-eater. I took them from her, and the zombie sobbed again, trying to reach for me in desperation. I did pity her. I pitied her condition and the loss of, what seemed to me, to be a perfectly lovely human.

That night, I arranged the objects from her pocket on my father's windowsill beside a candle. It was like a shrine to the woman who once lived, or that was my intention. I hoped that whatever happened to her spirit, that she was happy and free. I tried to make the mysterious rectangle play music or show me a face again, but I couldn't. I could only see the grid of symbols like an impossible puzzle to solve.

Before I fell asleep, I remembered the touch of her skin and the scent of her hair. It felt so unfair to have found a zombie so intact and attractive. How unlucky I was to be taunted by beauty; the very love and lust I would never experience in my fractured world.

14. Hannah

It was David who called my phone. Not to check in on me, or because he wondered where I was. He called me to gloat. He wanted me to know I was wrong about Tara. In the afternoon on the day of my abduction, she texted him and asked him to take her on a date.

He didn't know that his call, as it echoed from my pocket, was a glimmer of hope. He didn't know I couldn't physically answer or that if I did, my mouth was taped closed. He didn't know my captor would rush in, straddle me and grope my breast before confiscating my only link to the outside world.

I wept all night. I wept until the skin around my eyes was raw, red, and puffy. My tears drained into the wrinkles of duct tape until the stickiness remained only in my hair. But I didn't scream again. I didn't want to summon the boy. I could hear him in the room across the hall. He listened to opera, a musical choice that only assured me that he was a psychopath. I don't remember ever sleeping, just becoming weak and delirious, fading in and out of thoughts and consciousness.

In the black of night, I thought I saw the boy for a moment, barely a shadow in the dark of the hall. I felt his eyes upon me. I saw movement in his shoulder and elbow. One hand in his boxers. But it was only for a moment. I would never be sure if it was my own imagination preying upon my fear.

It was hard to tell when the sun rose; the room was always so dark. But I could see the color change through the cracks in the wood, blue to pink to orange to yellow. I thought of the world beginning its day. I imagined my mother waking up and wondering where I spent the night. I imagined Benton's friends and family learning of his death. Unless, I realized, the boy had hidden the body. Perhaps he was only presumed missing.

I needed to pee. For a while my general state of duress had kept the urge at bay. But after nearly a day, my body remembered its basic needs. I supposed the need would have arisen sooner had the boy provided me with any food or water. I wondered if I would have consumed anything he gave to me.

As if he could read my thoughts, the boy entered moments later, reigniting my panic. He had a cheerful disposition, devoid of the stress he carried the day prior. It was as though he had completely absolved himself of murder and abduction. He began to talk to me again in his bizarre language. I strained to hear him and to understand.

"Tet nelash i. Tet gibber go secrah. Fyfesha tet howald go."

It was like gibberish. It followed no rules I could comprehend. It was neither Latin-based nor structurally Germanic.

He set two glass vials down beside me. They were small and corked with black rubber. They contained an opaque orange liquid.

He reached for my face. I flinched as he pulled the duct tape down below my chin. He put his finger to his lips and hushed me.

"Journ," he said.

My throat was dry, but I cleared it and spoke plainly.

"I don't understand you."

He chose to ignore me and picked up one of the vials. He held in front of my face like a child presenting his show-and-tell.

"Please let me go," I said.

"Von relshavon," he continued, "Tet kaope imbal lea fur ume noya wi etsra, go leshel, tansal namityn skyntar."

He removed the stopper from his vial.

"What the fuck is that?" I asked him.

He downed it in front of me. He over-exaggeratedly rubbed his stomach and smiled.

"Von popi. Smek sich... Fufa tabolyn."

Von, smek, sich- Those words stuck out. They did sound like German. From Poppies? Maybe taste it... I didn't understand the rest. But, Poppies? Was he trying to feed me an opiate?

He picked up the second vial.

"Do you speak English?" I pleaded. "Please, I don't understand."

Again, he ignored me. He uncorked the second vial and pushed it into my face. I was not about to ingest mystery fluid willingly. But the boy grabbed my face and forced the glass tube through my lips. It clacked against my teeth and its contents spilled into the corners of my mouth and leaked down my cheeks. What made its way into my mouth, I promptly spit out. The taste of artificial citrus lingered in my mouth.

That made him mad.

"Hocha!" he yelled. He had used it once before. I assumed it was a swear.

He began to pace in front of me, speaking too quickly for me to catch his syllables. Clearly, my resistance had thwarted whatever his plan was. When his words came to an end, he crouched, red-faced and tearful. He was frustrated, it seemed by something larger than me.

My phone rang again from the other room. The boy perked up and left to investigate. It was David, this time to check in on me. I knew it was even without seeing the screen. It was rare for me to miss his phone call and not at least text him back. I hoped that it was the beginning of any search for me. If I manage to survive a few more days, I thought, I might even be found. But to survive, I needed food and water and preferably without time spent in a puddle of my own urine.

The boy returned shortly, scratching his head and leaning in the doorframe. He had acted like he had never seen a cell phone before, but I didn't understand how that could be true. Either way, he seemed to earnestly have no concept of how to answer mine. He appeared dejected and I decided to speak to him, despite our inability to communicate.

"So what was in the vial?" I asked him. "Rufie Sunny D?"

He looked back at me sadly and shook his head, but in a way that seemed unrelated to my question.

"I mean, you almost got me. You did the old 'See, I'm drinking mine' trick. It maybe would've worked if you served it in a glass instead of a suspicious test tube."

He continued to look at me like a disappointed little brother. He really was the last type of person I would have expected to be a murderous kidnapper, I guess mostly due to his age. It was easy, suddenly to see him as a person worthy of pity. I had studied the effects of trauma in school. I refused to believe my captor was born to behave in the way he did. But I couldn't delude myself into believing I could appeal to his better senses either.

"You're so young," I found myself saying aloud.

"Hoch nyr-fara vorden," he responded in a way I could tell was dismissive.

It sort of pissed me off. I shifted in my discomfort and found some bravery. He didn't look like he had his gun on him.

"These chains are cutting off my circulation," I said more loudly. "Also, I need to use the bathroom."

He did nothing.

"Hey, Fuckhead! You're not going to want to grab my boobs if I'm covered in my own shit! Bathroom! toilet, toilette, baño, um... latrina, doko... Please!"

He started to move, sighing deeply and reached again for his dreaded roll of duct tape. My anxiety rose again, triggering tears I didn't know I had left.

"Please No!" I cried.

But he returned to sitting on my legs and I heard the rubbery rip of tape. And in this moment of desperation and utter exhaustion, I stuck my tongue through my lips and made a fart sound.

He stopped what he was doing confused and batting his eyes at me with childlike amazement. A grin formed on his face. So I did it again and he began to laugh.

"You get that?" I asked him. I forced myself to smile, to look friendly. "Yes, poop, that's what I'm going to have to do eventually."

He didn't exactly understand, as evidenced by him choosing to blow a raspberry back at me. He laughed again as though we had found a game to play.

"Yeah, it's a funny noise."

"Hina i skampi von go," he replied and punctuated it with another fart noise.

It really was a universal language.

"But I actually really need to go." I motioned with my head towards the hall where I imagined the bathroom might be. "Toilet."

I watched the cogs in his head turn. It felt like he might've actually understood, but didn't trust me.

"I won't struggle," I said, though I wasn't sure if I were lying. "I just need the toilet."

"Esa portas? Ume lenshel go von gibber pram, und wi sheva pram."

"Toilet," I repeated.

"Toi-let," he mimicked and nodded. "Eya."

He left and returned shortly holding the keys to my shackles.

15. Lothryn

I was surprised when the siren asked to use the toilet. Dad had described the zombies as dead, so I expected them to cease bodily functions. But the more I thought about it, the less zombie physiology made sense. If they ate the flesh of the living, that flesh had to go somewhere. It stood to reason that their digestive tracts remained functioning. In which case, they likely pooped.

Furthermore, the siren had warm skin rather than cold, dead flesh. After chopping up Dad and Idola, I was well acquainted with the difference. The siren had a heartbeat, she had tears. She was emotive and seemed to genuinely think. Even still, I was afraid of her. I couldn't be sure what she was, even as nearly all signs pointed to her being a living human like me.

I had a theory, or maybe a hope, that she had overcome the virus; that she had unique antibodies that prevented her from becoming a zombie, or that she had been fighting it off for years. I wondered what would happen if I fed her the antidote; if it would cure her or reveal her true nature.

I wanted desperately for this to work. I wanted to be the hero that saved her life. It was so hard to keep her chained up. Every time she cried, I felt like a villain. Maybe deep down, I knew I was.

Aside from his stories about the fall of civilization, Dad also told me tales of far-off make-believe lands. There were elves and fairies, and knights and princesses. There were evil sorcerers and terrifying dragons that threatened the land. The villains were complicated and tortured; the heroes were impossibly noble and valiant. No matter what trials were put in their paths, the heroes would overcome stronger than ever. They were never emotionally wounded or traumatized beyond repair.

When I was younger, I aspired to be like the heroes in these stories. But as I got older, I began to understand that they were unfair standards with which to measure myself. Yet my childhood ideals remained, challenging me to remain positive through the most adverse conditions.

I danced the vial in front of her face. She looked unimpressed.

"It's tasty," I tried to assure her. "It tastes like... sweet oranges."

I tried to feed her the antidote, but she resisted and let the precious liquid run from the sides of her mouth and onto the floor. I became angry with her, and then, with myself. I felt foolish for thinking I could make her comply. I seethed as the antidote left orange stains in my bedroom's carpet.

Perhaps imagining cleaning the stains of the siren's excrement is what ultimately convinced me to take her to the bathroom.

I grabbed my rifle to make sure she understood not to try anything. She kept an eye on the barrel as I unlocked her shackles. She massaged her wrists and ankles, bruised in shades of blue and yellow.

"Come on," I said to her.

I stood guard in the doorway and ushered her in. She was slightly taller than me. She stared down at me with her dark eyes, searching with an utter lack of understanding. Then, modestly, she lowered her shorts and sat on the toilet.

She continued to stare at me, and I averted my eyes. Our silence was soon interrupted by the awkward and altogether human sound of her urination.

"Dad said only zombies speak the old-world language," I explained aloud. "But you seem too smart. I don't know what you are."

As her hand searched for toilet paper, I saw her eyes discover the blood stains around the base of the bathtub and clinging to the grout of the tile. It was my father's blood. I figured out how to be cleaner when I disposed of Idola. The siren reacted with some surprise and revulsion. When her eyes returned to me, it was with a renewed sense of fear.

She didn't fight me when I returned her to her shackles. She even held out her arms for me and allowed me to lock her up with a weary complacency that made me wonder if she had given up. She had circles under her eyes, her skin had lost some of its radiance.

"You look weak," I said.

Her arms were shaking. Her lips were chapped.

"Are you hungry? Do you need to feed?"

More tears welled in her eyes. She rubbed them against her shoulder. She said something, her voice scratchy and sad. I wished I could understand her. I cursed my dad for never teaching me a language I knew he was fluent in. I cursed myself for not pushing him harder.

"What do you need?" I asked. "Meat? Human flesh? Brains? Or do you eat regular food?"

She turned away from me.

"Hey," I insisted.

I mimed eating my own hand and then pointed at her.

"You want eat human?"

I saw sudden comprehension in her eyes. She nodded her head. She said something else and raised an imaginary cup to her mouth. I nodded back. At least that body language was universal.

I went to the kitchen and poured her a glass of water. But I had trouble deciding what to feed her. I reasoned that she had mimed a cup for water, but that she hadn't corrected me when I bit my hand. She didn't shake her head and mime eating a sandwich or use an imaginary fork. Maybe she was an intelligent zombie who still craved human flesh.

If I was wrong, if she was a survivor like me and I tried to feed her human flesh, I'd know immediately. She wouldn't eat it, and she'd look at me like I was a moron. But at least I would know.

I opened my freezer door. The heads of Idola and my father sat among boxes of frozen food. I could nearly feel their eyes staring back at me through the plastic bags. I didn't think I could stomach watching the siren chew on my father's face like a popsicle. So, I retrieved Idola's head and served it to my waiting captive.

16. Hannah

I don't know what I was expecting my mysterious captor to feed me. A dry piece of bread spotted with white mold, apple sauce, a bowl of macaroni and cheese. I imagined a styrofoam tray filled with the cheap food I ate at the cafeteria in middle school. Tater-tots, a dollop of ketchup, and a small carton of chocolate milk.

That isn't what he brought me.

Instead, he arrived in the doorway carrying a glass of water and a small black plastic bag; the kind I would expect to receive at a liquor store. It contained something heavy and oblong. I anticipated a rotisserie chicken or a cantaloupe. Granted, I hated cantaloupe, but I wouldn't turn it down if the alternative was starving. He set the glass and the bag in front of me like he was presenting me with gifts; like he was the servant and I was his queen in chains.

He backed away and returned to leaning in the doorway to watch me eat like a weirdo. I had to second guess why he wanted to watch me. Did he earn a fraction of trust by letting me use the toilet and now he was going to poison me? Why would he do that after chaining me up for an entire day and night? I reminded myself that I couldn't apply my own logic to the boy. He already had done so much I would never do.

I picked up the glass and looked at the bottom. I didn't see any residue. I smelled it. It smelled like water. I took a small sip. It tasted like water. Before I knew it, I drank the entire thing. I didn't realize how thirsty I was.

I looked from the empty glass and back to the boy. I wondered if I could break it and stab the base into his throat.

"Go von durqi," he said with a smile.

"Thank you for the water," I replied.

As soon as I reached for the bag, something just felt wrong. It was cold and icy. The crinkling plastic sent an odd chill up my finger. At first, I didn't know what I was looking at. The visuals entered my mind like scattered pieces of some terrible puzzle. I saw frosty flesh, matted blonde-white hair, frozen blood, an ear, and finally the piercing stare of a dead woman. Horror flooded my senses and crawled up my spine like a trail of stinging centipedes.

I lurched away from the bag, throwing myself into the wall, as far as I could get from what I saw. I didn't scream, so much as I heaved and gasped, pulling at my chains as my wrists and ankles bleed.

The boy scrambled to the bag and pulled it away from me. I felt no relief. My captor was standing in the doorway with a woman's frozen severed head in a bag. A woman he had undoubtedly killed.

"Who?!" I choked on my scream.

He looked panicked, apologetic even. He said something back to me, but I could hardly hear him as my tears returned. The new tears stung against my eyelids. Were they tears for the woman? No, I couldn't mourn her. I had no capacity for thoughts on the past. She was a promise of the fate that would likely befall me. I saw my own frozen head in a plastic bag.

Nausea overtook me and vomited. There was only the water I had just consumed, but I continued to dry heave in uncontrolled spasms on the floor. The boy was no longer in the doorway. He didn't return that evening, even as I loudly wailed.

I made noises I had never heard myself make before, deep miserable moans like the ones my mother made when my dad left. I hadn't understood her misery at the time, but I suddenly got it. It wasn't simply sorrow; it was fear and hopelessness, the complete lack of faith that the situation would ever improve.

In the dark of night, I stared up at the ceiling and listened to the silence of the stagnant room. I began to engage with a curious sense of peace.

"It's okay," a part of my mind whispered to me, "This is how you die. Everyone dies."

I remembered visiting Puerto Vallarta in Mexico. I was a scrawny eleven-year-old. The waves at the beach were intense. Daniella, Hector, and I stood at the shore and allowed ourselves to be hit by them. There was an undertow. We knew that. There was danger and that was part of the thrill. Wave after wave and we were fine. Just giggles and excitement. Then, came a big one. The undertow swept me deep beneath the wave. My eyes were open. I saw sand and bubbles and I didn't know which way was up. I was underwater for what felt like an eternity, long enough that my lungs started to burn.

And I heard my mind whisper, "It's okay. This is how you die. Everyone dies."

But then I surfaced. I was far from the shore and another wave swept over me. I surfaced again and struggled and swam. Daniella met me halfway and helped me to the beach.

Later I heard a man say that a boy had died on that beach, drowned in an undertow. I felt like an idiot because I knew it could have just as easily been me.

The reality of my impending death transitioned from a possibility to a likelihood. But it wasn't a certainty, I reminded myself. I could swim against the current and gasp for air as I breach the surface, or be tossed helplessly into darker waters, a victim to the tide.

I didn't know at the time that David had already started looking for me. It stood to reason after I wasn't answering my calls or using social media or returning to my home, but I was too preoccupied to thoroughly consider what my friends and family were doing on my behalf.

He saw the report of Benton Stuart's death in the news and texted me. When I didn't respond to something he knew I would respond to, he called my mother. My poor mother was worried. She hadn't heard from me and when David mentioned I might've seen the murder victim on the day he died, she assumed the worst.

David was never one to sit idly by and wait. He decided to walk to Benton's apartment from my house to retrace my steps. Tara offered to walk with him. She had a vested interest in what happened to me. David read this as evidence of her kindness.

They stopped outside the apartment complex and looked up to the fourth floor to a window obscured by newspaper and wooden boards. They wandered over to the side alley where the news reports had detailed it as the location of Benton's death. Everything was already cleaned up, though as they walked closer, they found blood stains on the concrete.

It didn't occur to David that walking onto a crime scene so soon after a murder could be seen as suspicious. Or that it might be under surveillance by a detective. Thus, he was startled when a tall authoritative woman approached from behind.

"What brings you here?" she asked them.

David jumped. He was jumpy when startled.

"Detective Lynn Jarvis, LAPD."

She flashed her badge.

"Fuck," said David. He also swore when he was startled.

"You don't mind if I ask you a few questions," said Jarvis. She was very type-a. A notebook was already in her hand.

"Shit," said David. "We're just looking for my friend."

"I assume you're aware a homicide occurred here barely over twenty-four hours ago."

Tara and David nodded with a sort of dumb innocence that immediately let Jarvis know they had nothing to do with the murder.

"May I see some ID?"

They fished out their licenses and she took down their information.

"Who's this friend you were looking for, David?"

"Hannah, Hannah Moreno. She's my best friend. I haven't heard from her and-"

"Was she one of Benton's clients?"

David didn't know what to say. He didn't want to get me in trouble for buying drugs.

"I'm only interested in the homicide," she assured him. "I honestly could care less if she was buying molly."

"Well, shrooms," said Tara.

"But, It was her first time," David quickly added. "She wasn't like a regular of Benton's. I don't know if she met up with him even. All I know is that she hasn't answered her phone since he was killed, and that's why I'm nervous."

He pulled up a picture of me on my phone. Likely the one where I'm dressed like a dinosaur for a Halloween party.

"I know it's too early to report a missing person," he said. "But I can't shake this feeling. This is her."

"It's not too early," said Jarvis. "Especially if her disappearance may be related to a murder. I'll keep an eye out for her. But, she'll probably pick up soon."

She gave Tara and David their IDs back and handed them her card.

"Please give me a call if you come across any information that you think could help."

Her eyes drifted up to the top of the building. The strange boarded-up windows were a conspicuous peculiarity; an eyesore that was out of place even in a worn-down yet functioning Los Angeles neighborhood where women walked their dogs in overpriced athleisure wear. Neither I nor my unlikely search party could fathom that it was my prison.

17. Lothryn

I decided my captive wasn't a zombie.

Her disinterest in eating Idola's brain was the final shred of evidence. To be honest, disinterest put it too lightly. The sight of the severed head terrified her. I felt bad for traumatizing her any more than I already had. And yet, her fear was confusing to me. If she were a survivor, she likely would have been well acquainted with the abundant gore in the outside world. She would have had to have killed to survive. She probably decapitated several zombies before I ever found her. It didn't add up.

I tried to remember the face of the man I had found her with, the man I had shot. I remembered he had dark, sunken eyes. I could have sworn he was decaying. He was a zombie, wasn't he? He had to be. I convinced myself it was the truth; the alternative was too horrific.

I spent the night thinking about a story Dad once told me. He used to tell me Greek myths before I went to sleep. A man called Tantalus was given the honor of hosting a dinner for the gods. But what meal was worthy of a god? Tantalus decided that the best way to show his devotion was to sacrifice his own son, Pelops, and feed him to the gods. If he was willing to kill what he loved most in the world, the gods would surely favor him. But the gods despised human sacrifice. They cursed Tantalus and resurrected Pelops. Pelops nearly got to live on Mount Olympus, but he was punished for the sins of his father and sent back to Earth.

The story had always made me think about resurrection. I thought of every life that had been taken by the zombie virus. I wished that the gods would breathe life back into humanity and let us live again. I wondered if something like that had happened to my captive; if life had returned to her body after years of walking death.

My father wasn't religious. He didn't instill in me the teachings of any god or gods. He didn't ever let me believe in magic and fairytales. But I loved to hear about any world more colorful, exciting, and full of life than my own. All I had was the bleak expanse of a hostile and dangerous ruined planet.

In the morning, I brought my captive food. Real food. A bowl of cereal, pretzels, I thawed some frozen fruit, I made beans. I knew she would be hungry. I set them before her on a tray with two glasses of water. I sat across from her and ate jam on toast.

She looked withered and hazy. Her cheeks were gaunt, her hair was stringy. I thought of unchaining her, but I was still nervous. And after what I had put her through, would she try to harm me?

She stared at her food like she didn't know where to start.

"I hope you like pretzels," I said. "I have pita chips too, but you seem like more of a pretzel person. And..." I added miserably, "you don't understand a word I'm saying."

She took a sip of water and nibbled on a pretzel. Her eyes were locked on to mine. I couldn't read her emotions. She looked shattered.

"This is insane," I muttered. I spoke to her again as if the more I spoke, the more she would understand. "Dad never said anything about survivors who speak the old world language. Maybe this is the big change he was talking about. What if everyone's cured, or brought back to life? Maybe nature or... the gods found a way."

I realized something, something simple, something I should have done before. It stood to reason that if she could make me understand "toilet," we could communicate in other ways. I pointed to myself.

"I'm Lothryn."

I poked my finger into my chest again. She stared blankly at me.

"Lothryn. Lothryn."

She cocked her head. I pointed to her.

"You?"

She looked stunned. And then, like a light went off behind her eyes, she replied.

"Mainaymisshana."

"Woah, That's a long name. Mainaymisshana." I repeated, pointing to her.

She shook her head and pointed to herself again.

"Hannah. Hannah."

"Hannah," I said. "Lothryn."

"Lothryn," she echoed. It was nice to hear my name on her lips. She said it again and leaned closer to me and spoke slowly. "Lothryn. Yura bahdpersuhn. Yura merderuhr." She pointed again and repeated "merderuhr."

I smiled back at her. "No, I'm Lothryn."

She exhaled deeply and slumped against the wall. She ate all of her pretzels. I knew she would like them.

I was struck by a sudden idea. The dictionary was still in my father's room. Now that I was confident she -Hannah- wasn't a mindless zombie, it stood to reason she could use the dictionary. We could write to each other. I could explain to her why I chained her up. Hopefully she would forgive me.

"Oh!" I said aloud. "I am an idiot!"

I bolted from the room. I grabbed the dictionary off my father's desk. I found pens and a pad of paper scribbled with my father's notes. More examples of a language he could have taught me. I ripped them out and returned to Hannah. She jumped when I reentered the room and pushed against the wall as I sat closer to her. I set the book next to her hand.

"Can you read this?"

I asked a little bit too loudly. I worried that she thought I was shouting. She didn't grab the book. She was frozen and shaking again. I picked up the book and flipped to find the word for understanding.

I showed her the word as I spoke it and slid my finger to the characters beside it that I couldn't read. Then Hannah said it, my word for understanding, nearly perfectly.

My heart raced with hope. For the first time since Dad died, I felt relief.

"This is great," I said. I'm not sure she understood just how miraculous it was that we could communicate. She was still so afraid of me. I hoped I could find the words to change that.

I began to write down my thoughts. I wanted her to know who I was, that I wasn't bad, and that I was sorry.

18. Hannah

The boy was called Lothryn.

It wasn't a name I had ever heard before, not that I expected it to be. It fit in with his fractured unidentifiable language.

He served me breakfast in the morning, an odd combination of food in bowls. Frosted shredded wheat with milk, hot beans and some sort of sauce, microwaved mushy pineapple and berries, and pretzels, as if I weren't dehydrated enough. To his credit, he brought me two glasses of water. This was all before an accompanied trip to the restroom to be sure.

There was an uneasy duality to Lothryn, I thought to myself as he served me with an innocent smile. On one hand, he aspired to be personable and project kindness, but other times he looked anguished and mad at me. And of course, he had killed at least two people and abducted me. And that was just what I knew of.

While I was interested in whatever chemical misfirings were happening in Lothryn's brain, I tried not to diagnose him. I recalled having difficulty with the concept after taking my first psychology class. My professor had introduced so many terms and conditions in just one semester and I was eager to apply what I had learned to the behaviors of me and everyone in my life.

"I think I have cyclothymia," I said to David one afternoon.

"How's that?" he replied flatly.

"I have days where I feel great, like I'm on top of the world and then, without any real reason, I crash. I feel sort of blah for another few days, and then I get over it."

David shrugged as he often did, with noncommittal indifference.

"I don't know. Sounds to me like you have emotions. I'm pretty sure peaks of joy and lows of misery are normal parts of the human experience."

"I don't feel normal," I told him. "I feel lost."

"Well, I don't think doing a self-diagnosis after one psychology class is a healthy way to find yourself."

I had to agree. My professor had advised against it as well. I wasn't a professional, I couldn't begin to understand Lothryn or his mind. I couldn't even determine what he was saying.

It was sort of amazing when Lothryn pointed to himself and said his name. I didn't get it at first, but he repeated and it was like a blindfold being removed. I felt like Jane Goodall after years in the jungle, finally grasping a lead on how to communicate with her gorillas.

"My name is Hannah," I said to him. He didn't understand at first and I realized my mistake. "Hannah," I clarified, "Hannah."

Lothryn smiled and it triggered something in me, a rage that had been brewing.

"Lothryn," I said to him. I had his attention. "You're a bad person. You're a murderer."

It didn't have the desired effect. He didn't know what I said, of course. He didn't even acknowledge my anger. He just stared blankly and shook his head.

"Ume," he said. "Tet Lothryn."

If my hands weren't shackled, I would have facepalmed. I sighed instead and fell back against the wall.

"Eh!" he shouted suddenly. "Tet von stamka!"

He stood and ran from the room. I heard him in the other room across the hall, rummaging and talking to himself. He returned moments later with a leather-bound book, a couple of pens, and a legal pad. He sat so close to me, like a gossiping friend at a sleepover. My heart leapt in my chest. I feared whatever new information he would bring me; what twisted clue would be added to the troubling circumstance of my captivity?

He opened the book and showed me its pages. I saw handwritten words in columns next to an unintelligible scrawl. His finger was on a row.

"Cindinscite," he said to me.

His finger moved to a word beside the scribble. "Cindinscite" was written clear as day in familiar Latin characters. Two soft C's, two short I's, a long I and a silent e, 'sındınsaıt. I visualized the phonetic transcription in my head. Beside it on the page, I saw what I believed to be the definition- Understanding, Comprehension.

"Cindinscite," I repeated as if it were my turn at the spelling bee.

"Von eyaka!" Lothryn cheered. He rolled away from me and began to write on the legal pad. No doubt, he wished to convey his thoughts to me in ways he hadn't been able to before.

Meanwhile, I was left holding a crude dictionary for some language I had never seen before. It began with a page on numerals. On the top of the left column, it read "Semaj-Kire." I presumed it was the name of the language. I checked the spine of the book. Sure enough, on a yellowed sticker, "Semaj-Kire Dictionary" was printed in Latin letters. I turned back to the first page. The middle column read "Roman Characters" and the right was labeled "English."

I scrolled down the left column and found characters for zero through ten followed by multiples of ten, then a hundred, a thousand, and a million. The symbols were abstract at first, looking more like a step-by-step drawing of a rising sun than a numeral, but I quickly discovered the logic behind the pattern. it wasn't complicated. In fact, it seemed to go out of its way to be simple. In this way, it felt incredibly modern and invented like Esperanto.

I began to flip through the dictionary of words. It was long, but not long enough to feel like a working language. There weren't many synonyms or words with layered meanings. It felt empty, unfinished and entirely unpoetic.

I looked back to Lothryn. His tongue stuck out of the side of his mouth as he wrote. I wondered if the dictionary was something he had created himself, if he had some deeply fractured personality disorder, if one side of him knew English and the other only spoke this language. I didn't believe he was a strong enough actor to so convincingly pretend he didn't understand me. And I couldn't help but feel curious about what he would write to me. I hoped that whatever he said, I'd be granted some answers, or at least some leverage that might lead to my escape.

But what Lothryn's note provided me with an utter absence of answers, and instead presented another curious assault of questions. I should've known this would've been the case when he handed it to me, brimming with the sort of sheepish excitement that reminded me of being asked out via note by a quiet boy in the seventh grade.

He handed me the legal pad and the translation began. The first thing I noticed was that his handwriting was nothing like the handwriting in the book. This didn't rule out the possibility to me that Lothryn authored the book. I had read about people with multiple personalities that had separate and distinct ways of writing. I found it fascinating. Yet, in the context of my situation, it was frustrating. Identifying the matching words was that much harder.

It took me close to an hour, but that was partially because I had to recheck Lothryn's words. Many were absurd and altogether, I had no idea what he was talking about.

"Hello," the note read. "Sorry I had to chain you up. I had no idea that you were a human like me. Sorry also for any harm I caused you. Please don't think that I am weird. My name is Lothryn Odris and I am seventeen. Before meeting you, I thought I was the only survivor of this horrible plague."

That was the first place I stopped. I wondered if there was another meaning besides "survivor" and "plague." There wasn't.

"Please answer my questions," the note continued. "And I will probably free you, but may still point a gun at you to be safe. Number One: are you a zombie?"

I stopped here again. I found it odd that, in spite of the brevity of the dictionary, there was a word for zombie- several words for zombie, actually- let alone that Lothryn chose to ask if I was one.

"Number two: If you aren't a zombie, why do you speak the old-world language?"

I assumed that's what he called English, but the question itself was nonsensical.

"Number three: Are there other survivors out there? Number four, just for fun: do you think I am a good-looking guy? I have not met a woman before. I have never been outside until recently."

That part, I believed. The house smelled more stagnant than any place I'd been before. And the way he looked at me, it was like I was an alien. When he touched my breast, it was with scientific curiosity.

"Also, sorry I tried to feed you a frozen zombie brain. Please write me back in my language. You are very smart and pretty."

I lowered the notepad from my face and found Lothryn looking at me like a puppy dog. I almost felt bad for him. Whatever was happening in his brain had twisted reality into make-believe. Perhaps worse, his assumption that I would have anything kind or romantic to say to him after he abducted and abused me was delusional.

I struggled to come up with anything to say to him. What was there to say to a person who lived in a completely fictional world? Somehow, I collected my thoughts, wrote them down, and began to work on the translation.

19. Lothryn

Dad had me believe that I would likely never meet another living human. He said he didn't want to get my hopes up. If it happened, he wanted it to be a miraculous and unexpected surprise.

"You cannot make plans for the future on the basis of wishes," he told me. "The truth is harsh, biting, or boring at its best, but it is kinder than the lies we tell ourselves in the long run."

Sometimes when he warned me, his eyes drifted away. It was as if his own wisdom resonated inwards or he was hearing his advice for the first time as he spoke it.

In spite of his words, I had always held on to hope.

I had imagined a number of scenarios where we would encounter other survivors. My favorite involved a caravan of gun-wielding vigilantes who had driven an amazing distance to pick off the remaining zombies and make the city safe again. They would find us and take us back to their utopian fortress that they built in the forest. It would be lush and picturesque like parks I had seen in books. There would be hundreds of people there, including girls and boys my own age. I would have friends and a future. It was the safest and most optimistic of my daydreams.

My most depressing thoughts included my father dying and me living far beyond his age. With no one to protect, I would wander from city to city finding desolation as far as the eye could see. I'd run out of antidotes and fall victim to the airborne virus. In my dying breaths, I would see another survivor scouting through the rubble for a survivor like me. She would comfort me in my final moments before shooting me in the head.

I hadn't anticipated finding Hannah, and certainly not as quickly as I did. But I saw her as my salvation, my reason to live in a world that wanted nothing more than my death.

She read my note. I was unable to tell from her reactions what she thought of me and I couldn't wait for her response. She was very smart. She thought for a long while before starting to write back. Then, I watched her use the dictionary to begin her translation. It took a while, but she kept at it. She ate her cereal and her beans. She left the hot fruit untouched. That was fair. I wasn't a huge fan either, but Dad said I was supposed to eat it to prevent scurvy. I preferred fruits and vegetables when they were fresh, but that was rare.

I began to doze as I watched her work. The flutter of her eyelashes was entrancing. Her face, full of concentration was somehow comforting. A ray of sunlight trickled in from the window to kiss the curve of her cheek.

I hadn't noticed I fell asleep until I was awakened by a sharp tap on my face. I didn't know what hit me. I saw Hannah, still seated against the wall. She gestured with her head to something at my feet. She had folded the paper into an airplane and flown it into me. I picked it up and grinned at her. I interpreted her creativity as a positive omen for what was to come.

I unfolded the paper to find a letter written in Semaj-Kire. Her handwriting was delicate and precise, occasionally with scribbles through parts where she messed up. And while sometimes she put words in the wrong place, it was legible.

"Hello. Free me please," it read. "Hoping I good answer your questions. One, I am not zombie. I am person."

I sighed in relief, not that there was much of a doubt anymore. Still, it was nice to see it in writing. I didn't believe a zombie would have the ability to write anything coherent at all, much less, answer a question.

"Two, I talk language I born to talk. Three, I am not certain what you ask. You killed my friend."

I had to read the last sentence again. I prayed she didn't mean what I thought she meant. I heard the bullet I had fired echo again in my brain. I saw the man fall.

"That man," I said to her. "He wasn't a zombie? He was a survivor, like you?"

She didn't understand, or maybe she did. She stared into me, her eyes unwavering. I saw the man's face in my memories. He wasn't decaying. He was alive and full of fear.

"He was a man," I said.

My face became hot, my eyes filled with tears. I pushed past the denial my mind created to protect me. I was angry. It welled up in my heart and pooled with nausea in my stomach. I ground my teeth. I found, with some surprise, that I directed my anger at my father along with every bit of information he withheld from me.

"You see, if my father had just taken me out into the world with him, I would have known what to look for! I would have known how to identify survivors! I would have known how to distinguish them from the infected!"

Hannah flinched with my every move. I was a killer. I punched the wall. I killed an innocent man. I punched the wall again. I felt the drywall crack beneath the quilt. I sank to my knees, pleading my case to my nervous captive.

"It isn't fair. My mom made him promise, but he didn't have to keep that promise, not this long anyway! I'm a man now. If he hadn't kept me inside, I'd feel like one. I hate being such a child!"

I sank my head to the floor. I didn't want Hannah to hate me. But how could she not? I killed her friend. What if they were more? What if she loved him? I couldn't imagine she would ever love me, or even like me. I had ruined that chance with one careless impulsive moment.

"Hannah, I'm so sorry," I pleaded. "Tell me how to make it right."

I looked up at her. She looked less fearful now. I had made myself as small as possible in front of her.

"I'm so sorry, Hannah."

She held out her hands towards me. With sun rays cascading down her shoulders, she looked like a merciful goddess; or like Andromeda chained on the rocks.

"Lothryn," she said. Somehow hearing her say my name only made me sob harder.

"Lothryn," she repeated. And then she said it, in perfect practiced Semaj-Kire. She was so smart. "Let me go."

I gulped down my misery to look at her. For a moment, I wondered if I had imagined it, if my hopeful brain was lying to me.

"Please," she added. "Let me go, Lothryn."

There was no question. I knew what I had to do.

20. Hannah

"Clar tet bara."

I had memorized the phrase. I strung together the words to the best of my understanding: Clar (allow) tet (I) bara (free.) I held out my shackled hands to Lothryn.

He was in shambles. My note had triggered an emotional response in him I hadn't anticipated. I couldn't follow what he said, but he yelled and cried. His state of duress was unsettling. My mother had once told me, "There are few greater dangers to a woman than a wounded man." It was a phrase that stuck with me and one I was sad to learn was more often true. But when Lothryn dropped to his knees and pleaded with his face to the floor, he was so defeated. For the moment, I didn't feel threatened.

"Clar tet bara," I repeated.

Lothryn raised his head to look at me. The blue of his eyes was intensified by his contrasting puffy red eyelids. The way he gazed at me, it was both haunting and hopeful.

I couldn't tell if he understood me at first. He was nodding, either to me or himself. Slowly, he rose to his feet and walked out of the room. I heard him sniffling across the hall. He took some time, talking quietly to himself. He carried his rifle when he returned, but he didn't aim it at me. Instead, he knelt and pulled out his keys.

"Und byngyn," he said. It was one of the words I had looked up. Byngyn meant sorry. Und was some sort of modifier similar to "so" or "very."

I didn't know how to take his apology. I certainly didn't accept it. I wasn't even sure, in the long list of things he had done, what specifically he was apologizing for. Maybe all of it.

He was still sniffling as he released me from my shackles. He offered his free hand to me, but I didn't take it. I would stand on my own.

Just as before, he guided me to the bathroom. Only this time, he stood further away. He gestured to the door. I cautiously reached for the doorknob. He nodded and let me close it for privacy. It was progress, at least.

I sat on the toilet and looked around the room at my options. There was no lock on the door. The locking mechanism was hammered out of the center of the knob. I turned to my left to view the window. It was unlike the other rooms' in that it had metal bars rather than wooden slats. The window was heavily frosted and nailed shut. Obstacles aside, it was too small for me to squeeze my body through.

I began to consider if there were any weapons at my disposal. There was a toilet brush and a plunger, a toothbrush in a plastic cup by the faucet. Nothing seemed viable.

I flushed and walked to the sink. The drawers were full of hotel soaps, travel-sized toothpaste, and shampoo. There was a razor, but not the sort that could cause any real damage. I opened the medicine cabinet and found some antihistamine and a bottle of aspirin. There was enough in there that I could make Lothryn overdose. I imagined feeding him all twelve pills at once would do the trick, or at least make him vomit. I opened the bottle and poured it into my pocket. I wondered how easily I could crush them into a powder and slip it into his food.

I replaced the bottle and closed the mirrored door. I considered breaking it so I could stab him with a shard. Too noisy. He had a loaded rifle just outside the door.

I caught my reflection. I looked exactly as I felt; drained, out of sorts, and steps away from death. I had deep circles beneath my eyes. My skin looked almost colorless. The wound on my forehead was swollen and scabby. But I wasn't dead yet, I reminded myself, I had managed to survive and I would continue.

Lothryn knocked on the door. I didn't want to make him angry.

"Just a moment," I said.

He didn't understand me. The knob turned, he opened the door, and poked his head in cautiously. He caught me looking in the mirror at my head wound. He grunted and gestured to the shower. He mimed washing his forehead.

I looked down into the bathtub. There was blood on the tiles. I shook my head and waved my hands.

"No thanks," I told him. "I'll be stinky."

He seemed to figure that out and gestured down the hall, away from the room I was being held in. That was surprising; I had assumed he would take me back to my shackles, not that I was complaining.

However, I wasn't sure where I was being told to go. I wondered if I was being prodded into some kill room, if I would find the body that belonged to that frozen head. But it was only a living room. The walls and windows were covered in wood and blankets like the bedroom. It was dark and dotted with the same cheap candles I'd seen at the liquor store. There was a couch and coffee table, a dining nook in front of what I guessed was a kitchen, and a map of Los Angeles covered with pins, string, and marker, the kind that might belong to a conspiracy theorist on a TV show.

Lothryn gestured to the couch. I sat. It was nice to sit on something soft.

"Ekaya," he said. "Go von tam tak. Tet esa tsun smekyn."

Then, he walked into the kitchen. My eyes found the front door, or what I believed to be the front door. There was a peephole. There were also five locks: a door chain, a swing guard, two deadbolts, and a lock on the knob. They all face inwards though; I wouldn't need a key.

My heart began to race. I envisioned myself running to the door. I knew I could reach it, but I wouldn't be able to unlock every lock before Lothryn turned the corner and blasted me with his rifle. I saw my blood splatter against the door. It was too risky. I would need time.

What I wasn't aware of, was that time was ticking down for Lothryn. Detective Lynn Jarvis was in the apartment complex speaking with residents about the murder of Benton Stuart. She had with her a police officer named Clemmons. They were standing outside the apartment exactly one floor below us talking to mild-mannered tenant, Dante Morales.

"I didn't know what I heard at first," he said. "These punks like to come and shoot off fireworks sometimes, but this time, I was like, man, that was really loud."

"You didn't look outside your window to see what the sound was?" asked Jarvis.

"No ma'am. Like I said, you get used to certain sounds. It was loud, but I didn't know that someone just got killed. Trust me. I would have called you guys right up."

Jarvis thanked him for his time and left him alone. She was pissed; she had no leads.

"I swear, this place is like a community for shut-ins and hoarders," she said to Clemmons. "It's insane that a gun went off and no one looked outside their fucking window."

"Yeah, the lot next door was clueless yesterday too," said Clemmons.

"Any word on the Landlady?"

"Zero. Won't answer her door, won't answer her phone. Residents report not having seen her for a while."

"Can't imagine how when everyone's so observant," Jarvis spat. "Brilliant. I can add her to my list of missing people."

She entered the stairwell to head to the top floor, but stopped. A familiar set of voices were ascending towards her.

"David Greer," she said.

Her voice echoed down the stairs, stopping David and Tara in their stride.

"Oh shit," he replied.

"And his girlfriend?"

Tara and David exchanged glances.

"Uh maybe she's my girlfriend," said David. "She's my friend and she's a girl."

"We're fucking," said Tara.

"We haven't come up with a label for it yet," added David.

"I'm happy for you both," Jarvis replied flatly. "Why are you here, again?"

It wasn't a coincidence. Nothing, as I would discover, was a coincidence. The night prior, Tara had told David about an app she had on her phone. All she needed was my phone number and she could track my cellphone's location. It sounded too good to be true, but David was happy for any opportunity to find me.

He was afraid, though. He told Tara that he didn't want to find only my cell phone; he wanted to find me. And when he found me, he wanted to find me alive and unharmed.

"I'm looking for my best friend," he said to Jarvis. "Tara's app said she should be here on the corner. Top floor.

"That's the one with the boarded up windows," said Clemmons.

"Interesting," said Jarvis. Perhaps she wasn't out of luck after all. "I'm headed to that apartment right now. If your friend or her cellphone is in there, we should know soon enough. But I'll need you both to stay back."

I was still in the living room on the couch. Lothryn had returned to me with a bowl of off-brand marshmallow cereal. He had the dictionary on his lap and was trying to converse with me. He pointed to a word on the page, "Opeyist." He slid his finger over to the English word.

"Delicious," I read.

"Delicious," Lothryn repeated with a grin and shoveled cereal into his mouth.

He reached onto the table, uncorked a vial of orange solution, and drank it in one gulp.

"What is that?" I asked him.

He pointed to a word in the book, "Belshavon - Antidote."

"Antidote for what?"

"Etsra," he replied. He took the dictionary and showed me the word next to the English word, "Virus." He then flipped the page and showed me, "Namityn - Zombies, Infected."

A new thought entered my mind; What if Lothryn really believed in zombies? What if he had convinced himself that they were real? Or what if someone else had convinced him they were real?

I couldn't reply to him. We were out of time. Detective Jarvis's fist banged on the metal gate outside Lothryn's door. I heard her muffled voice.

"LAPD."

My heart leapt.

"Pram hine sprell?" Lothryn asked me.

Jarvis banged her fist again.

"LAPD. This is detective Jarvis, I'd like to ask you a few questions."

Lothryn stood with his gun, defensively like he wanted to protect me.

"Von gan namityn?"

"Namityn," I remembered the word. He was asking if it was zombies. I shook my head. I grabbed the dictionary and flipped through until I found the word "Nera - People, Humans."

"Nera," I said to him. He ignored me, continuing to walk to the door. "Nera!" I shouted.

Lothryn put his finger to his lips, but I heard people outside. I heard salvation.

"Help! Please!" I yelled.

"Open up!" a man's voice yelled back.

Lothryn turned back to me, his eyes were wild and angry.

"Von wremund, war von hanor. Hannah, gan ume nera! Gan ume amdan!"

I couldn't follow. I couldn't listen.

"Help me! He has a gun! Please!" I cried.

"Wissahn!" Lothryn shouted back.

He put his hand over my mouth and snarled at me. I felt the barrel of his gun push into my sternum. The banging on the door became more intense. Clemmons was a big man with enough force to kick down the door. But he wouldn't be fast enough to save me if Lothryn decided to pull the trigger.

21. Lothryn

I felt as though Hannah and I were developing an understanding. I believed that, in time, we would have developed a way to communicate. In time, she would have discovered I wasn't a bad person. In time, she would have rolled away the curtain of my father's deception. But that's not how the story went for us.

There was a thunderous banging on the metal gate outside the apartment door. A voice rang out from the other side, speaking the old world language. I jumped. Whatever it was, it sounded aggressive.

"What did it say?" I asked Hannah.

I reached for the dictionary. I needed her to know what I was asking. But the banging rang out impatiently and I left the book where it sat. There was strength behind the hit. The voice spoke again, intimidating and forceful. I stood slowly, gripping tightly to my rifle.

"Are they zombies?" I asked her.

I paced slowly towards the door. Behind me, I heard Hannah flipping violently through the dictionary's pages.

"People," she said to me.

I shook my head at her. It didn't sound like people. I heard scratching footsteps against the cement. There were at least three of them. They spoke in horrible whispers to each other. One had a deep bass voice. He was probably a big one.

"People!" Hannah shouted more loudly.

I wished she wasn't so noisy. I didn't know how she could be so sure. Zombies had tried to enter the apartment before. It always sounded like banging. And zombies spoke in the old-world language. What did she know that I didn't? I wondered. I was about to try to ask her, but she shouted again, this time in her language. A shiver of rage shot up my spine.

I spun around to hush her. The banging continued. I heard a heavy clank and the creaking of metal. The gate wasn't complicated to bypass. It slid easily from its frame even when locked. Now only the door stood in the invaders' way. There was no way they were human; I was certain of that. Humans would not be so bold.

"Hannah, these are not survivors!" I tried to tell her. "They're not people!"

She ignored me and yelled past me. She wanted them to hear her. It was the opposite of what we needed to do as survivors. If we were quiet, the zombies couldn't tell anyone was home. Why did she not know this?

"Quiet!" I pleaded with her.

A loud percussive thud echoed from the door. They were going to get in. Still, Hannah screamed. I didn't know what else to do. I put my hand over her mouth and pushed her against the wall. Fear, again, returned to Hannah's face.

"I need you to be quiet!" I said to her. Her eyes kept looking to the door with wanting. "It's like you want them in here. You're summoning them..." The thought overtook me. Everything that Dad had said to me about the beautiful intact zombies that led men to their deaths. "Like a siren," I hissed at her.

I couldn't think of any other explanation. The girl called Hannah had deceived me. My face felt hot with rage, I could have screamed, I could have cried. I couldn't believe I had been so foolish. If I died that day, overwhelmed by zombies in my own home, the one I had survived in for seventeen years, it was a fate I was certain I deserved. I was blinded by hope and beauty, the very things Dad warned me about.

Rage blurred and warped my vision of Hannah. But I couldn't strike her, I couldn't pull the trigger on my gun. I twisted her bruised wrists and brought her to her knees. She cried in pain, but I couldn't care. She had brought zombies into my home. They would break the door and make my safe place no longer viable.

I dragged her through the hall and threw her into my bedroom. Adrenaline surged through my veins. I felt strengthened by my rage. I put a single shackle around her ankle. It was all I had time for. She was yelling and sobbing again when I slammed the door.

From my father's room, I grabbed the pike that leaned on the wall next to his door. There was no time for anything else. I could hear wood splintering. The zombies would be upon me soon. I rolled into the bathroom and crouched, waiting for them to come. I would have the element of surprise. I would skewer the first one I saw.

Dad often told me about times out in the field where he was surrounded by zombies. He said his heart would be pointing, but he'd reach this place of calm. All of his neuroses and anxiety would flood upwards out of his body and it would be like he was seeing himself from above. There was only him and the zombies; a lone warrior standing against monsters.

I heard the door crack open and I felt it. No thoughts clouded my mind. I had clarity. I was a warrior.

The zombies crept into the apartment. The light from outside cast harsh lines into the hallway. They moved slowly, but I knew they would come to me. Hannah was a siren, crying out to them. They were drawn by her voice and I would use it to my advantage.

I heard them whisper to each other again, harsh and decisively. They were like single-minded animals.

I saw a large shadow in the hall. I heard the creak of the wood floor under the weight of a hefty boot. It was two steps away, then one step. I lunged.

I heard a gunshot and the sound of glass breaking behind me, but I wasn't hit. I followed through with my lunge and stabbed the beast through his chest. I pushed with such force, I felt it break through ribs and crunch the thin wood of the hall cabinet door on the other side. But that wouldn't kill a zombie. I grabbed the rifle next and shot him in the face.

The blast was deafening in such an enclosed space. I didn't look at my victim. I knew there were more. I knew they could swarm at any minute. I ducked and strafed into my father's room. I kept my back against the wall. My ears were ringing. I reached into my pocket, fished out another bullet and loaded my rifle again. No horde was coming for me. Hannah was continuing to wail from my room and pound against the floor.

I replayed what had just occurred in my mind. The zombie was wearing dark blue. He fired a gun. Could zombies use guns? Dad never said. But it did shoot at me, which meant it wanted me dead. Whatever it was, it was an enemy.

I poked my head into the hallway. I could see my victim. He wasn't moving; he was pinned to the wall by the pike. His slumped head was a mess of gore. Blood was dripping down his body and pooling beneath his sprawled legs.

His gun had fallen from his limp hands and skidded into the baseboard, too far away from me to safely reach. I could hear another zombie speaking loudly in the other room, panting like she was struggling for breath. And there was another voice, that sounded distant and mechanical, like the voices sang from my cassette player.

I decided that I would need better cover. If another zombie was carrying a functioning gun, I couldn't risk being shot in the open. Dad said he would use anything to his advantage. He would roll behind cement road blockades and regroup in sewer tunnels. He said the zombies were stupid and didn't think to check outside their field of vision. I dropped and rolled beneath my father's bed.

My heart was racing. I could feel it more with my chest against the floor. It felt like my entire body was being lifted with every pulse. I wondered if the bed was shaking. But I kept my eye on the door. Any movement and I would fire.

As I waited, my eyes drifted to my father's closet. the artifacts from his life that I had only barely begun to investigate. If Hannah had been who I hoped she was, she could have helped me uncover the mysteries of his writings. I tried not to let it distract me.

I heard the floorboards creak in the hallway. A second one was coming. It seemed slowed by the body of the first, but it didn't stop to cannibalize the corpse. Dad said that happened sometimes, depending on the "freshness" of the zombie. The floorboards creaked closer. It was funny to rely on the sounds of my home that had only been an annoyance before.

My hunter stopped in the doorway. I couldn't see it clearly. I had partially obscured myself with the quilt that hung from the bed. I needed the zombie to take one step into the room. And that's where I made my mistake. I underestimated the creature's intelligence. I saw movement. A shoe dropped into my field of vision and I fired. It bated me. It threw a shoe into the room to make me waste my shot.

A hand pulled the quilt aside. I saw a face and a gun. She was a woman, older than Hannah. Tall, fearless, and intimidating. Her hair was pulled back in a ponytail. There was no sign of decay on her face, only anger.

She yelled at me and gestured with her gun. I didn't know what to do. I dropped the rifle and pushed it aside. She continued to yell and point her gun. Why wasn't she biting me? If she wasn't a zombie, why wasn't she speaking the language my father assured me any survivor would know? Everything was falling apart.

She began to back away from me slowly. It seemed like she was demanding I come out from under the bed. I didn't want to come out. I wanted to stay there and make myself as small as possible. I wanted to put my hands over my ears and make everything that didn't make sense crumble into ashes and float away.

There was a noise like I had never heard before, a jet of air but hard to describe. It was followed by a slump to the floor. The woman that had found me was dead. I saw the exit wound in her forehead leaking blood on the carpet. Her eyes were open, still holding a look of surprise. Then I heard a voice, angelic and sweet.

"Lothryn Odris?" she said. "You're safe now. You can come out. I'm here to help you."

I felt a lump in my throat. There was a young woman in the room. She spoke my language fluently. I saw her boots step past the predator she had slain. She crouched and ducked her head so she could see me. She took my breath away. She was beautiful. She looked like the women I had seen in magazines.

"I won't hurt you," she assured me with a sweet smile.

She held out her hand to me. It felt suddenly like it was only me and her in the world. I couldn't hear Hannah screaming from the bedroom anymore. I gladly took her hand and pulled myself out from under the bed.

Her hair and eyes were dark. She wore deep red lipstick and dangling earrings. She tucked her pistol back inside her motorcycle jacket.

"You're safe now," she said softly.

"Who are you?" I asked. "Where did you come from?'

She smiled at me again. I felt like I was waking up from a bad dream.

"Don't worry," she said. "I'm here to help you."

I felt tears well in my eyes. In the days since my father died, I had suffered through the loss of being cared for. I forgot how much I needed it. The way the woman looked at me, I believed she promised it.

"You're safe now," she repeated.

She held out her arms and took me into her embrace. I couldn't help but cry. She hushed me and stroked my hair.

"Thank you," I whispered into her ear. "What do I call you?"

"Tara," she replied.

Then I felt a sharp sting in the side of my neck. But the pain subsided quickly. My vision began to blur and darken.

"You're safe now."

I heard her voice again, but I couldn't be certain she had said those words again. I sank into the comfort of her arms as I drifted off to sleep.

22. Hannah

He didn't kill me.

For a moment, I thought he would. I saw Lothryn blinded with anger. He torqued my bruised and bloodied wristed until my knees buckled and I sank to the floor. I had forgotten how strong he was. He pulled me through the hall and forced me back into his bedroom.

I continued to scream. I needed the police to know I was there. Lothryn shoved me to the floor and clamped a shackle around my ankle. But I wasn't fully restrained. He left me there and slammed the door behind me.

For a moment, it was like nothing had changed. I was back in my prison with all the progress I had made with my captor undone. but in moments, I heard the front door crack open and the police officers enter with heavy footfalls.

"Come out! Hands where I can see them!" I heard a man shout.

Then, there was quiet, a whispered communication between the officers. Officer Clemmons took point and moved carefully down the hall with his pistol drawn, the same way he had many times before. But he couldn't anticipate Lothryn, who had been trained by his father to survive. He didn't expect a cornered killer wielding an ornamental pike from a renaissance faire.

I heard two gunshots. The first was cacophonous. The second was even louder. In the moment, I didn't know what happened. I had grown up wary of police officers. They would frequent the areas I lived in to break up celebrations on account of noise violations. Occasionally, they arrested neighborhood boys for suspected gang activity. I saw them as invincible with every weapon at their disposal and bulletproof vests. So I assumed Lothryn was dead. I couldn't believe a boy, no matter how strong, would win against a cop.

But then, I heard Detective Jarvis speak into her radio. Her voice was panicked, shaken by whatever she had just seen.

"HQ, we've got an officer down. Requesting immediate backup. Suspect is armed and dangerous."

"Hold position, Detective," the radio crackled back at her. "Back-up will be arriving shortly."

My heart sank. Lothryn had killed one of my potential saviors. And it occurred to me, all too suddenly, that a police presence did not mean a guaranteed rescue. Officer Clemmons and Detective Jarvis were just regular people. Clemmons was taken by surprise and murdered. Jarvis was succumbing to anxiety. I realized I still might need to save myself.

"I have a hostage here," said Jarvis.

"I have two units within six minutes of you," replied HQ.

Six minutes? A lot could happen in six minutes. Lothryn could kill the detective and me in less time than that.

"Six minutes," Jarvis echoed my thoughts. She sighed loudly. "Copy."

I heard her turn on her heel and walk down the hall. She knew, just as well as me that she had to neutralize the threat on her own.

"Hello Sir? My name is Detective Lynn Jarvis." She spoke with forced bravado. I could hear her uncertainty and her fear. "I'm with the Los Angeles Police Department. You have killed a police officer and kidnapped a woman. In less than six minutes this place will be swarming with LA's finest. You may either surrender peacefully to me now, or surrender your fucking life!"

I heard a creak of the wooden floorboards in front of my door. For a moment, I wondered if she would enter my room. I worried that she would and that Lothryn would shoot her in the back of her head. But she didn't. Instead there was another moment of silence.

Then a thump. Then a gunshot.

"Got you, you fuck!" I heard Jarvis say.

I thought that meant Lothryn was dead, but Jarvis continued.

"Now drop the weapon and come out with your hands up!"

I knew Lothryn couldn't understand her. For a moment, I thought about yelling just that. Then I asked myself why. Why would I do anything to protect him? And realized I felt sorry for him. Whatever had made him into the person he'd become, it wasn't his fault. Whether or not he survived his encounter with the police, that would be part of the tragedy. People would cheer the death or incarceration of a murderer without taking into consideration how a seventeen-year-old boy came to be one.

"Alright, nice and easy, now," said Jarvis. "Come out with your hands up."

I heard more creaking in the floorboards and then a sound I couldn't place. A harder thud rumbled the floor and I wondered if Lothryn had tackled her. But why wasn't there another gunshot?

Then came a woman's voice. It was so soft, I could barely hear it.

"Lothryn Odris? Tet ynca felet. Von encali. Tet von tak fur secrah."

I could hardly believe my ears. What woman was speaking the same language as Lothryn? How was that possible? And why did the voice sound familiar?

"Tet ume noya go."

Her voice became even quieter. Lothryn was speaking with her, but I couldn't make out what they were saying, not that I could understand either of them.

"Tara?!" It was David's voice. "We shouldn't be in here. Hannah?!"

I couldn't believe he was there. His voice was like a warm blanket. And I was immediately worried for his safety. I called his name, my voice breaking through my tears.

But he didn't come to me. There were more footsteps, steady and fearless, belonging to at least half a dozen more people. And then the person I least expected to see opened my door. There was Tara standing in the doorway peering down at me. She wasn't sympathetic and she didn't rush to my aide. She looked at me with a sort of cold intrigue.

"The girl is unharmed," she said.

A voice I couldn't make out spoke into an earpiece.

"Understood," she said. She walked towards me and crouched. She had Lothryn's keys and she unlocked my shackle. As she did, I watched a man in a black suit walk out of the other Bedroom with Lothryn draped over his shoulder. Two more men walked in with cardboard boxes and began to collect anything and everything from the room.

"What's going on?" I murmured.

"We're here to take you away from this place," said Tara. "Are you alright?"

She asked me like she was reading a line. She didn't really care. Why was she there? I nodded dumbly as she helped me to my feet. I could see Detective Jarvis on the floor being slipped into a body bag. I was walking before I knew it. The air and my mind both felt foggy like I was in a dream.

"Did I hear David?" I asked her.

"Yes, he's here."

She walked me through the hall. There was blood all over the floor. A body bag was in the bathroom next to a broken pike. My eyes swept past it and I found David in the living room, beyond a stream of crisscrossing men in suits.

"Hannah! Oh my god."

I ran into his embrace. I knew he would search for me, I just couldn't believe he would find me so soon. I cried into his shoulder.

"I was so scared for you," he told me. "And I didn't know why! I can't believe you're here. I'm so glad I found you."

"Thank you," I managed to say. "Take me out of here please!"

Tara's voice rang out again. She was notably unmoved.

"She'll have to go with Agent Cooper," she said. "He'll make sure she gets the attention she needs."

"Umm, okay," said David. He was even more confused by Tara than I was. "Can I go with her?"

"There's a car downstairs. We'll meet her down there."

"Okay," said David.

I felt a hand on my elbow. A sharp-faced blonde man I presumed to be Agent Cooper was pulling me away from my best friend. In hindsight, I should have insisted that I stayed with David. But I was so willing to believe my nightmare was over. I was willing to believe Tara despite the mystery of who she truly was. And David, understandably wanted answers. Who was the too-good-to-be-true woman who found him on a dating app?

"See you soon," said David. He smiled at me as Agent Cooper led me out the door into the warm air.

But I never saw him again.

The company Tara worked for didn't like loose ends. She apologized to David moments after I left them behind. He assumed the apology was for deceiving him. Then he felt Tara's silencer against his heart and the agents unrolled another body bag for my best friend.

Like Tara, Agent Cooper was all business. His grip on my arm was tight and unpleasant. There was a black car with tinted windows waiting for me outside the apartment building. I had expected an ambulance or maybe a medical technician on standby. Didn't Tara say I would be getting the attention I needed? There weren't even camera vans.

Agent Cooper opened the back door. "Get in."

I frowned and did as I was told. There was a woman in the backseat seated beside me. Her long legs were crossed in a black pencil skirt and black high heels. She wore dark sunglasses, had red lips, and a shock of white hair sprouting from her widow's peak. She flicked her cigarette out the window and rolled it back up. Then, the car took off.

"Wait," I croaked. "I thought we were waiting for David."

"They'll take him in a different car," said the woman.

She had a hybrid accent, German and English. She enunciated every word. I found her unsettling. If I had been rescued by my abductor, why did I still feel scared? She turned to me and smiled. It was a fake smile, like Tara's; the sort you would receive from a frenemy at a cocktail party. It lacked any empathy for what I had just endured.

"When I was in grade four, this little boy called Phillip had a crush on me," she said. "But he didn't know how to express it. I, of course, had no idea that him chasing me, calling me names, and punching me meant that he actually desired my company. Nor did I, when, after months of bullying he tied me to a tree with a jump rope and stuck his hand down my leggings."

I stared into her. I had no idea why she would tell me a traumatic anecdote, especially in my given circumstance. She shrugged at me.

"Hmm... Not even a smile? I was hoping you might relate."

I didn't believe her. She was callously toying with me.

"Who are you people?" I asked her.

"Well, you can call me Agent Hutch," she replied coyly. "Josephine, Jo, Dr. Jo- I am a doctor. I actually am not sure who's driving right now; I only know about half of their names."

I opened my mouth to interrupt her, but she talked over me.

"-And I know that's not what you were asking, but I'm giving you the answers I can. Hell, you might be able to figure it out yourself. I know you've been to our website."

I scrunched up my face. Delphi House Publishing, that place in the strip mall. But that's not what they were really. Clearly, they were some sort of government entity.

"Where are you taking me?" I asked.

"I can't answer that either," she said. "But I assure you, Hannah, when we get to where we're going, you'll be privy to more information than you ever wanted. For the time being, sit back, enjoy the ride and your blissful ignorance while it lasts. And help yourself to a water."

I spotted the bottled water in a cup holder on the floor between the seats. I didn't reach for it. Instead, I stared at it with the same skepticism I felt towards anything Lothryn offered me. I had traded one prison for another, complete with darkened windows, and dangerous company. I stayed silent for the rest of the ride.

23. Lothryn

Dad said my mother had hair like spun gold. She had big green eyes and a wide joyful smile. He said her laughter was melodic and infectious. She liked to hold me in her arms and sing songs with made-up lyrics by the window. She had a quick wit and could make up convincing stories without too much thought. Dad said he had trouble telling when she was lying. She was good at lying while he was only ever honest.

I never saw a picture of her. Dad didn't have any pictures of her, but I didn't think it was odd. He didn't have any pictures of himself either, or any of me as a baby or a child. We didn't own a camera. Cameras were a casualty of the apocalypse.

The image of my mother existed as an assemblage of ideals in my head. When I dreamt, I swore I could see her face clearly, but when I woke up, I never remembered what I saw.

I dreamt of her again when the woman called Tara put me to sleep. I saw her in a room I had dreamt of before, the laboratory where she worked. Dad told me the story of how the apocalypse began so many times, I had constructed many recurring locations. I saw tall white shelves with glass doors, chrome-colored refrigerators, lab coats, and beakers.

Mom wore a mask over her nose and mouth, goggles, and a cap to cover her hair. She shared the space with another woman, a colleague. It was a detail Dad sometimes left out, but it was an important one. She was the one who released the airborne virus. It was by accident, but was an accident that doomed the world.

My mother left the lab and walked down a dark hallway. She passed doors sealed shut, with access restricted beyond her clearance. She shuddered as she went by; the sounds of deathly coughing, wheezing, and inhuman hissing echoed from the other side. I found myself moving from watching her like an observer to physically following her down a twisting path.

She took me to a place I had never seen before. I couldn't tell if I was indoors or outdoors. I felt oppressive walls beyond where the space fell off into darkness. Beneath a spotlight, there was a blackened tree surrounded by crunchy ashen leaves. My mother walked towards it, dropping her mask and goggles. Her golden hair fell to her shoulders. Her lab coat bled into a gown. There was a single red apple on one of the branches, impossibly alive on the dead and withered thing.

She outstretched her hand towards it and picked the fruit. But wasn't for her; it was for me. She crouched and rolled it along the floor. It stopped and collided against my bare feet. But I didn't pick it up, I was distracted. A long crimson python was snaking around the trunk of the tree. It ascended to a height above my mother.

"Keep her safe," my mother said to me.

Then, the python sunk its fangs into her neck. Blood spilled over her white dress and I felt myself falling backwards.

I saw bright circles passing overhead. I heard wheels scraping against cement and people speaking old-world language in hushed panicked tones. I didn't know if I was still dreaming. the world felt foggy and dark.

I found myself in the presence of my father. I was crouched beside him holding a machete. Dad had his rifle in his arms. We were in an abandoned store, or what I imagined a store to be. The floor was flecked green tiles. We were between two aisles sparsely stocked with junk food. I was happy, happy that Dad finally trusted me enough to take me outside.

But Dad didn't look happy. He was annoyed with me.

"You shouldn't be here," He snapped at me.

"Why?" I asked him.

"Because this is my world," he said. "This is where the zombies live. You were never supposed to see the things I've seen."

There was a screech and hiss in the next aisle. I crawled to the other aisle. I saw daylight shining through the big glass windows. Cars drove by outside. I stood.

"There's nothing there," I said.

"I'm sorry," Dad replied.

I turned to face him. He was a naked corpse, cross-hatched with bloody lines in every place I had sliced him. His intestines dripped from his wounds. His eyes were sunken horrors. He aimed his rifle and fired a bullet into my chest.

I lurched. The pain felt real. My eyes shot open and I realized all too suddenly that they were already open. I felt pressure against my eyelids. They were being held open with silver wire tools. I was strapped to a metal table surrounded by people in masks and medical scrubs. My heart began to race, I knew I was truly awake. I could feel the cool metal, the weight of some contraption strapped to my head; I was blinded by a silver-hooded light with three bulbs blasting into my face.

I began to struggle and yell, and the people scrambled, rushing to hold me down. I felt a sting in my arm on the inside of my elbow and I drifted out of consciousness once again.

I saw Hannah. We were sitting in my bedroom together. But it was different. I was restrained and she was standing over me with a handgun.

"What are you?" she asked me.

I answered, but I couldn't understand the words that came out of my own mouth.

"My mother warned me about boys like you," she said with a snarl. "You look innocent, but you're actually monsters. I'm a human and you treated me like a toy."

I tried to apologize, but again, my words were muddled.

Hanna shook her head at me with disappointment.

"Eat," she said. "Let's see what you really are."

I saw a bag on the floor, frost-bitten and wet. It wasn't the bag that held Idola's head, this one held my father's. I shook my head. I could never.

"Then I know what you are, Lothryn Odris. You're a coward."

My eyes opened again. This time they actually opened. I was in a bright room on a squeaky cot. I sat up. The room was square with unfinished walls. It had a gray door with a rectangle of black glass at face-level. It was quiet.

"Hello?" I asked no one.

I put my feet on the cold cement floor. I had a headache. There was a bottled water and a chocolate bar on the floor. The chocolate bar had nuts and caramel inside. I ate it first and washed it down with the water.

"Hello?" I asked again.

I wondered where the beautiful woman was, the one who spoke my language. I wondered if she had ever really existed. I checked the door. It was locked, of course.

"Hello!" I yelled.

There was a buzz that emanated from the door. The knob turned and I stepped backwards. An older man entered wearing a lab coat and carrying a clipboard. He smiled at me uncomfortably and gestured with his hand for me to sit on the bed.

"Who are you?" I asked him.

He seemed to ignore me and gestured with his hand again. I already didn't like him, but I complied. The bed springs squeaked beneath me. The man held his clipboard out in front of him and adjusted his glasses.

"Hello, I am Special Agent Gomez," he struggled to say to me. His pronunciation was odd and choppy. "I just need to ask you a few questions to make sure you are feeling well."

"Sure," I said. "I have many questions for you as well. For instance, where am I?"

He ignored me again.

"Are you experiencing any respiratory issues such as a sore throat, sneezing, runny nose, or loss of smell?"

"No," I said.

He had a pen connected to the clipboard by a string. He used it to mark down my response.

"Are you experiencing body aches, vertigo, or an irregular heart rate?"

"No."

"When you interacted with Hannah-"

My ears perked up. What about Hannah? What happened to her?

"Did you feed her anything in an attempt to cure her of her presumed condition?"

"I tried. And what do you mean presumed? Was she or wasn't she a zombie?"

Agent Gomez wrinkled up his face. I realized he had no idea how to speak my language. He was reading from his clipboard. He only knew "yes" and "no." He started reading the question again.

"When you interacted with Hannah-"

"Yes," I said.

"Great," the man replied. He seemed genuinely happy to hear my answer. "Lothryn, I would imagine you have a lot of questions. Follow me and we'll see to it that they're answered."

"Of course," I replied. "And then I'll take a shit on your face."

Agent Gomez had no idea what I said. He stupidly smiled and nodded as he opened the door into a dimly lit hallway. I followed him and felt like I was stepping into my father's story. Lab workers and men in black suits bustled through the corridor, each granting me a passing glance as they went by. Whoever these people were, I was important to them and I intended to find out why.

24. Hannah

The car parked in a gravel lot beside a warehouse somewhere in an industrial part of downtown Los Angeles. I tried my best to look around, but I couldn't place where I was. Los Angeles was home to hundreds of worn-down warehouses even after housing developers started converting them into overpriced lofts for trust-fund babies.

There was nothing distinctive about this particular warehouse, other than it was occupied. It had a security officer working in a booth between two automatic gates topped with spiraling razor wire. There was a graffiti-covered overpass and a view of abandoned overgrown train tracks. I didn't get to see much else, as an agent tugged at my arm and led me towards a rusty steel door. Josephine Hutch lingered in the lot to light up another cigarette and chat to a man in a lab coat.

"Where's David?" I half-murmured, though I had given up on hearing an honest answer.

It was dark inside, but from what I could tell, construction on the facility was only partially finished. We walked past some rooms that looked entirely modern with clean chrome and white walls. Others had dirt on the floor and plastic drop cloths hanging from the walls.

The agent took a sharp left into a room that reminded me of a cafeteria, complete with lunch tables that had been converted into makeshift workstations. The room was full of attractive young women in black suits. I was reminded suddenly of the webpage I had found for Delphi House Publishing and the rows of smiling headshots I had scrolled through. The women shot me sideways glances and whispered into each other's ears.

"That's her?" I heard one say. "I thought she would be blonde."

The door on the other side of the room opened into a courtyard. We passed a few chain-link cages with their contents obscured by vinyl weave. I could hear the sounds of people coughing and struggling to breathe, much like the man I had encountered in the basement of the strip mall. A few heavily armed agents drove by us in a golf cart before disappearing through a set of automated double doors down a glossy white hallway. Behind a thick glass wall, a woman in a gasmask threw canisters of explosive orange mist at a human-shaped dummy while her colleagues took notes.

We departed through a smaller side door designated with a sign that read "restricted." After a maze of narrow gray hallways, I was gestured into a rectangular room that resembled a room in a hospital. There were two beds with a curtain hanging from an I-beam dividing the two. I could only see the end of the other bed, but I could distinctly make out feet beneath the fuzzy blue blanket that informed me it was occupied.

"Wait here for Doctor Roberts," the agent told me.

Then, he left and closed the door. I heard an additional click which made it apparent I was locked in. There was not much else in the room to speak of. A small metal tray on a stand held a few canisters of sanitary napkins, gauze, tongue depressors, and cotton swabs. On the wall opposite the occupied bed was a framed poster with a picture of a boat in front of a sunset. It had a quote beneath it that read, "The question isn't who is going to let me; it's who is going to stop me." It was an odd choice for a medical setting.

After a moment, my curiosity got the best of me and I poked my head around the curtain. The bed held an old woman with a long silver braid. She wore a hospital gown and had an IV stuck to her arm. Her eyes were closed and she was breathing rhythmically. I assumed she was asleep. But as I turned away to give her privacy, she began to speak.

"My condolences," she said. Her voice was thin and crackled like a campfire.

"I'm sorry," I said. "I didn't know you were awake."

I turned back to look at her. She hadn't moved. Her face stared up at the ceiling. Her eyes were clouded and gray. I couldn't see her pupils.

"You're a sweet girl," she said to me. "You'll never lose your kindness, but you will become calloused. You'll have to. You won't be able to rely on the boy forever."

"I don't know what you're talking about," I tried to say politely. "Do you know who these people are? Do you know what this place is?"

"This is where change happens," she said. "The people are all ghosts."

"Okay." I started to get the impression she wasn't entirely sane. "Well, hope you feel better."

"You didn't ask me," she replied quickly. "Knowledge is a strength. It's your strength. You must always question."

"I don't know what you want me to ask."

"I offered my condolences," she explained.

It hadn't registered with me that I needed to inquire further. And, given the circumstances, condolences felt somewhat appropriate. I was, after all, taken from one unnerving circumstance to another. I hesitated to learn why an old woman in a sparse and windowless hospital room felt pity for me.

"Alright. Why did you say that?"

"Because," she said. "You have experienced loss. Loss that you know, loss that you have yet to know, and loss you would never know."

I sighed. More bad news.

"Well, thank you," I said. "I'll pull through. I'm stronger than I look."

"I saw your brother die," she said.

I felt a pang of anger rise in me, but I pushed it back down.

"My brother's not dead," I said to her. "I don't know where he is, but he's not dead."

"His corpse lies in an ashen field. He was troubled by darkness. Flames took him. Hector lit the match himself."

My heart jumped. She knew his name. How did she know his name? It wasn't like my family records were a secret; a creepy underground agency would definitely have access.

"You're just trying to fuck with me," I spat at her. "It's not going to work."

The old woman didn't respond. Instead, her breathing returned to heavy exhales and her eyes fluttered to a close.

The door opened. A woman wearing scrubs entered carrying a clipboard and a small canvas bag. I didn't wait for her to get settled.

"What was the fucking point of that?" I demanded.

"Excuse me?" replied the doctor.

"The haunted old woman telling me my brother's dead?"

"Oh."

The doctor settled, ignoring my hostility. She pulled out a few pill bottles from her bag and turned back to face me with a smile.

"I'm sorry you had to share a space with Ruth. We were hoping she'd stay asleep. Don't pay her any mind. She spouts nonsense."

"She knew my brother's name," I said defiantly.

"Well, sometimes she gets something right, but mostly she's been a disappointment. It's par the course for her kind."

"And what kind is that?"

The doctor hesitated. "I'm not here to answer questions. Most things I won't even know the answer to. I'm just here to check you out before you talk to Agent Hutch."

"I already talked to her," I said. "She didn't answer my questions either."

"She will when she sees you again. Can you open up for me?"

I shrugged and opened my mouth. She put a depressor on my tongue and shined a flashlight into my mouth. She then swabbed the inside of my cheek and collected the sample in a jar.

"Can at least you tell me what you're checking for?" I asked.

"We just want to make sure Lothryn didn't get you sick," she explained. "And there's something else. Actually, something I should ask you."

She hesitated again and looked at me as if I should have known what she was about to ask.

"Were you and Lothryn ever intimate during your captivity?"

The laugh escaped my mouth before I knew it was coming. Intimate? What a weird way to phrase it. Even if he had forced himself on me, the act would not have been intimate. The woman didn't even blink, she just stood there, awaiting my response.

"You're asking me if the person who chained me up, threatened my life, and tried to feed me a severed head became intimate with me?"

"More unusual things have happened," The doctor replied.

"No!"

The doctor raised her eyebrows and recorded her response.

In spite of the doctor's shortcomings, she treated the wounds on my wrists, ankles, and forehead. With gauze wrapped around my wrists, I was reminded of some of my brother's favorite professional wrestlers. We used to watch it together and cheer on the bad guys. I refused to believe he was dead. It wasn't an option. I just didn't know whether to trust the doctor or the theory I had concocted in my own head.

After she finished, another agent in a black suit arrived to collect me and take me down another hall. There was a wall of cinder blocks to my right and unfinished wood to my left. We stopped by a door where two metal folding chairs were left for us.

"Have a seat," the agent commanded.

I did as I was told. He sat next to me, he had on his holster. He pulled out his cell phone with his other hand and began to play a mindless video game. I got the impression I would be there for a while.

"Can I use your phone?" I asked him. "I'd really like to call my mom and tell her that I'm okay."

He shook his head.

"There isn't any service in here," he told me.

I was serenaded by incessant video game sound effects for another fifteen minutes before the agent paused to listen to a voice in his earpiece. He stood and used his id card on a scanner beside the door and opened it for me.

A ribbon of smoke ascended to the ceiling from the end of Agent Hutch's cigarette. She was sitting at a desk beside a tabletop microphone, a reading lamp, an ashtray, and some scattered files. Fluorescent light spilled in from the window to her left and a dark mirror sat on the wall opposite her face.

"Come in," she said. "They've already started."

I stepped in and heard the door click behind me. There was a chair on the other side of her desk. I took my seat carefully.

"They get you all cleaned up?"

I nodded.

"Good."

"What is this place?" I asked.

"Oh, just your run-of-the-mill government and privately-funded corporate research facility," she said.

She held up a binder crammed with paper. It was beige with a logo with a red medical snake wrapping around a black tree. At the top it read, "Vaughn & Lachland Group," at the bottom, "Project Delphi." She set the binder back down.

"You know, I've never met Vaughn or Lachland," said Hutch. "I bet they play golf."

I caught movement in the bright window. On the other side, I saw a room opposite to the one I was sitting in. In Hutch's Position sat Tara. Her hair tied up in a bun, in glasses and a business suit, she looked a far cry from the glamorous vixen that stole David's heart. Across from her, sat Lothryn looking just as confused as me.

"That's Lothryn," I said.

"Yes. Yes it is," said Hutch. "Actually, funny story, his name is Isaac. Isaac Carpenter."

25. Lothryn

The man called Agent Gomez led me to a door in a dark echoey space. His shiny black shoes clopped percussively on polished cement. He carried a handgun in a holster on his belt. I had half a mind to wrestle it from him.

He used his identification to open a lock before turning the handle and guiding me into a smaller room flooded with sickly fluorescent light. There was a large mirror on the left wall and a large black desk between two chairs. A woman in a black suit was seated in the chair facing me. I nearly didn't recognize her at first.

She was Tara, the woman who had drugged me and taken me to this place.

The door clicked shut behind me. I felt uneasy, like a captive. I was torn. On one hand, Tara spoke my language; she offered me comfort. On the other hand, her actions had led me to a place where I endured horrors. I wanted to trust her, but a large part of me felt more attached to Hannah. In my brief time with her, I felt we had developed a connection. I wondered if Hannah screamed to warn me about the people that were coming; they could have been bad people. I was naïve to assume that people surviving the apocalypse, by nature, would be good.

"Have a seat," Tara instructed. She didn't give me complete eye-contact. She was tapping her fingers rapidly into a flat glowing screen.

"Why?" I asked her.

She looked up, cocked her head at me, and pouted innocently.

"So that we can talk."

"Why did you bring me here?" I specified. I folded my arms.

"So that we can be safe. So we can talk. Please sit."

I did as she asked. The table was empty aside from a silver basket filled with bright red apples.

"Are you hungry?" Tara asked me, catching my eyes. I shook my head. I couldn't eat; my stomach was in knots.

"Do you live here?" I asked her. "Do you live in this dark fortress?

She paused thoughtfully. I was perhaps more poignant in my word choice than I even intended to be. A strand of hair came loose from her bun and she quickly tucked it behind her ear.

"It's not all dark," she said with a half-smile. "And a fortress is a good name for it. It might just keep us safe if everything goes to hell. But no, I don't live here. But I feel like I do."

I had no idea what she meant. Hadn't the world already gone to hell? Why did she keep tapping her fingers on her screen? Was she writing?

"You did something to me," I said to her. "Back at my apartment, you stuck me with a needle, which I think made me sleep. Why did you drug me to take me here? It makes me feel nervous about trusting you."

She set her screen down. She reached out to me. Her fingernails were lacquered red like the skin on the apples. I felt her warm hands touch mine. She smiled warmly.

"I was worried about that too," She said. "I want you to trust me. My-" she hesitated, searching for an appropriate word, "Elders were concerned with you learning the location of this place. It's a secret. They're not certain they can trust you yet. That's why we have to talk."

In spite of myself, I relented that the logic made sense. And yet my mind flashed to the visuals I had seen between dreams. I remembered the bright lights as my eyes were held open. I remembered people speaking in the old-world language.

"How come nobody except for us speaks this language?"

"Why do you think?" she challenged me. "I can tell you're very smart, Lothryn. You must have theories."

I would have preferred she just told me, but she seemed generally curious in my answer. That's what I told myself at first. But as I struggled, she reveled in my discomfort. It was like she wanted to watch my understanding of the world fall apart.

"My father spoke of a change," I said. "Maybe it happened earlier than he thought it did. The zombies evolved to become intelligent like people."

I knew my reasoning was a stretch even as I said it. Tara considered my words and emitted a slight chuckle. She pulled her hands away and returned to her device.

"I'm very impressed," she said before quipping, "Mostly with your father, though." It was a slight I didn't yet understand, but it annoyed me regardless. "Did he ever mention what would have caused this change, a cure, perhaps?"

"Dad didn't tell me a lot of the details. I was hoping he would soon. I was hoping he would see me as a man."

"But he had you drink an antidote."

I ran my hand through my hair. How did Tara know what my Dad did or didn't do? I supposed it was logical that any survivors would have been familiar with the antidote. I shrugged off the question.

"Yeah, the orange stuff."

"And what was in that?" Tara asked.

She leaned in closer. I could see the words on her screen. She was writing in old-world language. She wasn't reading from a script, though. Unlike Agent Gomez, she knew what she and I were saying.

"I don't know what was in the antidote."

"You don't know?" Tara narrowed her eyes at me. "How do you not know?"

I shrugged.

"He just brought it home with him," I explained. "He collected it from a big vat at a hospital."

Tara rolled her eyes and sighed.

"No he didn't."

I scowled. "Yes he did. That's where he brought the little vials from. Why would I lie about that?"

"Oh, I know you're not lying."

She was leading me. But what was she leading me towards? I had a strange feeling of déjà vu that hurt my head to think about.

"Are you talking about my Dad?" I asked. "What reason would he have to lie about that?"

Tara cleared her throat. She looked to the window as if there was something beyond her reflection. She was listening to someone I couldn't hear. I watched the cogs turn in her mind. She turned back to me with a different demeanor. She was no longer smiling; she was cold and predatory.

"Have you ever heard the name Erik Carpenter?" she asked me.

I shook my head. It hardly sounded like a name at all.

"What about Isaac Carpenter?" she pressed.

I shook my head again.

She clasped her hands and rested her chin against her fingers.

"I'm afraid this will all come as a surprise to you. Are you ready to hear the truth?"

I didn't necessarily trust that Tara was interested in telling me the actual truth. Nonetheless, with my eyebrows aching from a constant knitted furrow, I nodded silently. I would listen to her "truth."

"Excellent," she said. "Now, where should I start?"

26. Hannah

Lothryn was exhausted and miserable. He looked as if he had aged a year since I last saw him. I couldn't hear the conversation he was having with Tara. But they seemed to be able to communicate just fine. Hutch was listening in with an earpiece. I could tell because she occasionally paused and looked off at nothing in particular or at the two-way mirror. She had said that Lothryn's real name was Isaac. I didn't know why that mattered. No matter what his name was, it didn't change the things he had done.

"He's not actually a bad person," said Hutch. She caught me looking at Lothryn. I must've been scowling.

"He didn't hold you hostage," I said.

"Of course. But that was hardly his fault. He had an unusual upbringing."

She shook her head at something she heard in her ear. There was a small silver button on her tabletop microphone. She pressed it and leaned forward as she spoke.

"This isn't working, Farris. Break him down."

Tara turned to Hutch and gave a slight nod. I watched her posture shift and the kindness leave her face. I recalled my first impression of Tara at the bar with David. She had drilled me for information. It seemed so long ago. But, sure enough, there she was: an actual interrogator. And she wasn't wielding finger guns anymore. I could see a real gun strapped to her belt.

Tara leaned towards Lothryn. She said something to him and I watched him break. His lower lip started to tremble and tears began to stream from his eyes.

"Isaac's father was a nut-job," explained Hutch. "Erik James Carpenter. He's an aspiring science fiction and fantasy writer. He moves to Los Angeles to pursue his dreams. You know the type."

I shrugged. My dad used to say that you couldn't throw a rock in Los Angeles without hitting an idiot transplant with a dream.

"He meets this young actress," Hutch continued. "They think they can help each other out. He writes, she acts out his characters. Naturally, they bone. Nine months later, she pops out Isaac, but she panics. She doesn't want the baby or Erik anymore. She wants her career; she takes off." Hutch took a long drag of her cigarette. "Here's where things go south. Erik feels like an utter failure. He lost his girl and he's never sold a book. Little baby Isaac is the only thing in his life that doesn't feel lost. Being the nut-job that he is, he decides to combine his passions and raise his son under the impression that he is living within one of his sub-par post-apocalyptic sci-fi novels. Bizarre."

Hutch raised her eyebrows at me. Bizarre was an accurate word. I didn't know what else to say. I had questions, but Hutch appeared compelled to tell me the whole story. She was tickled, as if she were gossiping with a friend at brunch.

"Erik calls his Lothryn, which means beloved in his kooky made-up language. I'm sure you're familiar by now with the language. You saw that Semaj-Kire Dictionary, right?"

I nodded.

"Semaj-Kire is Erik James backwards," she said with a laugh. "Add another check in the egomaniac column. Erik renames himself Eramice Odris after his favorite character. He's valiant and heroic. He leaves the house every day with a gun strapped to his back. He tells Lothryn he's off to kill zombies and scavenge for supplies. Really he's off to go work at the shitty liquor store. You might've even seen him. It's the very same one in your neighborhood."

Of course I knew the creepy man who worked at the liquor store. He was dead behind the eyes. I supposed I understood why.

"Meanwhile, Lothryn's left at home for years, too terrified to even look out a window."

Lothryn's face was bright red. He was drenched in tears, gesturing wildly at Tara. His entire belief system was imploding. And suddenly, I felt a place in my heart open for Lothryn. I pitied him. He wasn't raised to live in the existing world.

"It's amazing the power a parent's words can have over their child," said Hutch. Her crystal eyes twinkled in the fluorescent light. She was captivated. "He's still digging his heels in. The backfire effect is powerful, but the walls are breaking and the roof is caving in. It's fantastic to see."

Lothryn clutched his head as though he were in physical pain. I wasn't fantastic to see, as Hutch put it; it was tragic. Lothryn has been an experiment to his father for his entire life. Now, he was the subject of Agent Hutch and her team.

"Are you a Christian?" Hutch asked me.

I winced. I dreaded hearing the reason for her query.

"Kind of," I said. "I was baptized, but I'm not practicing."

"Do you remember when you found out there was no Santa Claus?"

So that was all. I did remember. My sister told me and my brother. It wasn't a big deal for us. We still got presents.

"I was ten," said Hutch. "I had a big imagination. I still do. My parents were worried I was going to believe forever. It's devastating the older you are. You feel foolish and deceived."

Lothryn was in ruins, his face buried into his arms on the table as his back convulsed. Slowly, he reached out to the basket of apples beside him. He grabbed one and bit into its crisp flesh. Tara turned to the mirror and made a face. She was suddenly unsure of what to do.

"Don't worry, just give him a moment," Hutch said into the microphone before returning to me.

"How come she speaks his language?" I asked.

"She studied it. We've had Erik's manuscripts on file for a while. We brought in Specialist Farris to understand the structure of the language so she could communicate with Lothryn. She's a linguist."

I gasped.

"That's such bullshit!"

Hutch cocked her head at me, confused by my outburst.

"Everyone said there weren't any jobs in my field," I grumbled.

"Oh. Well, she's important to our work. She's not just a linguist, she's a psycholinguist."

"A what?"

"It's the interdisciplinary study of psychology and linguistics," Hutch explained. "Psycholinguists specialize in the ways in which language is represented and processed in the brain. I read your file and learned about your studies. You don't have to choose between psychology and linguistics. I'm surprised no one ever told you this before."

"Yeah, me too," I said. I turned back to Tara. I hated her even more than I did before. " So, why does she need to communicate with Lothryn?"

"I'm glad you asked," said Hutch. "There was an element in Mr. Carpenter's work that initially drew us to his study. Did Lothryn try to feed you any of his "antidote," the orange beverage?"

"Yeah. I didn't know what it was. It tasted like a powdered juice, like Tang."

"Very astute," she replied. "It was Tang."

She pulled a slender pamphlet out of her binder and handed it to me. The cover said, "Tang, ETSRA prevention and you." It was six pages, stapled on the spine. I flipped through it as Hutch spoke.

"You see when man first ventured into space travel, there were many unknown factors that proved dangerous to our astronauts. Among those dangers was an airborne parasitic virus that came to be known as ETSRA. Though our company was only budding back then, we used our resources to create a practical and delicious temporarily preventative oral "antidote" called EXtros. Tang, as it is more commonly known, was first launched on February 20th 1962 with the Mercury Project and has been protecting astronauts from contagions ever since."

I gave the pamphlet back to Hutch. With each new piece of information, I began to question her sanity. To use her own word, it was bizarre.

"What does the virus do?" I asked.

"In layman's terms, it kills us, and reanimates our corpses so that we react to stimuli in cannibalistic rage. Zombies."

I didn't know how she could say it with a straight face. I could imagine how I looked, endlessly confused. Hutch didn't wait for me to absorb everything she said. She pulled out a thick manuscript bound by brass fasteners and sat it in front of me.

"Imagine our surprise when this much-guarded information was detailed extensively as the premise to Erik J. Carpenter's sci-fi novel, Awakening: The Twilight of Eramice Odris."

I read the cover page as she said it. Hutch extinguished her cigarette and folded her arms with an air of self-satisfaction. I couldn't understand why.

"This is fucking joke," I said.

She smirked.

"I know, I know. Everyone's a visual learner."

She reached beneath the table and flicked a switch. Suddenly, a poured in from the other two-way mirror. I wasn't sure what I was seeing at first. There were people milling about in a large empty room. There were probably twenty of them. They were moving slowly and mindlessly, lurching and sick.

I stood and walked towards the mirror. I wasn't interested in believing Hutch and her weird stories. But there was something uncanny about the way the people were moving. As I got closer, I could see more details in their filthy clothes and bloodied skin. Some could have easily been made up to look like a zombie. It could have been realistic make-up. I had watched enough tutorials online to support that theory. They didn't look any less alive than the horrific man I had seen in the strip mall basement. And yet others were walking on rotten legs with exposed bone. A particularly nightmarish woman had hardly any skin on her skull, her hair was a collection of spider web-like wisps, her eyes and lower jaw were missing. Yet she was still moving.

"There's a reason we're called Project Delphi," said Hutch. "Pythia, Cassandra, Nostradamus... Oracles have existed throughout history. Many wrote or created art without truly understanding the inspiration behind their work. After finding his work, Erik was theorized to be such an oracle. So we've monitored him. We've watched and waited."

She stood to observe the tragic monsters alongside me. I saw her face in the reflection, glowing in the darkness.

"If the virus becomes airborne here on Earth, as predicted in the work of Mr. Carpenter," she continued. "The result would be catastrophic. Like I said, our antidote only temporarily staves off the virus. What we're looking for is a cure. We were hoping that Erik would complete his series, his prophecies, safe in his own little world. The thought was that any interference by us would disrupt this delicate natural process. Unfortunately, our oracle kicked the bucket before he could point us to a cure. It is our deepest hope that before he died, Erik disclosed a formula to his son."

I felt her breath on my neck. She put a firm hand on my shoulder.

"To be frank, the notion that Lothryn may have passed this information on to you is the only reason you're still alive."

A zombie smacked his palm on the window right in front of my face. A handprint of thick dark blood oozed rivers on the glass.

27. Lothryn

It was a funny thing to be told the truth, finally, after being fed nothing but lies. I, of course, responded to Tara's words with resistance. But, that didn't last very long. My father's tower of deceit was imperfect; it depended nearly entirely on my dependency on him and my foolish belief that he was, by nature, consummately honest with me. I was always in denial. I explained away every shred of evidence that threatened the reality of the world I knew. Any sound of joy I heard outside was a misunderstanding. Dad's resistance to teaching me "English," as it was called, was done out of love for his son.

My anger, too, was short-lived. Just as I discovered during my outbursts with Hannah, I couldn't stay angry with my father for very long. I had too many fond memories in his company. Where he denied me life, he also provided for me. He was affectionate and nurturing, entertaining and fair. Tara referred to my continued reverence as a form of Stockholm syndrome. I was unfamiliar with the term.

I bartered with the information as well. What if it was all a test? Or perhaps I was still dreaming? Maybe I could accept that was actually Isaac Carpenter, but what did I have to give Tara in order for her to tell me another sweet lie?

She was unrelenting and cold. As I wept more than I knew I could, she hammered me with questions to break down my defenses.

"Didn't you wonder?" she asked. "Didn't you wonder why the refrigerator worked but you had to use candles around the house? Why the water still ran hot and cold? Why the toilets flushed? In an apocalypse?"

"He said they were on a different system!" I said. "I didn't know."

"You didn't know or you didn't think?" she pushed.

"I didn't know! I didn't think! Why would he lie?!"

I wallowed in depression at greater length. I was so tired. My father used me to fulfill some part of himself that he couldn't satisfy. Now, in a room with a manipulative agent, I was being used again. It was increasingly obvious. She needed me for a reason I didn't yet know, and she wanted me at the end of my rope so I'd be grateful when she offered me a hand. I couldn't look at her, the woman I once believed was a radiant miracle of hope. Her motivations didn't save room for my well-being. My tears dripped off the table and onto my jeans.

"Lothryn, Your father didn't lie about everything." Tara's voice was suddenly softer. I realized she hadn't spoken for a while. She had been standing there for a long time just watching me cry. She had tactics yet again. "Your father saw things in mind. Visions of a probable future. He was desperately trying to explain something that he himself didn't fully understand."

I didn't know how to respond to her. My arm slid out the table and pawed at the fruit basket. I took an apple and bit into it. It was so fresh. It had been such a long time since I had fresh fruit. Dad had brought home apples a few times in my life. He said red apples were tricky. It was harder to tell with them if their flesh would be sweet and crunchy or gross and mealy. He said green apples were safer, tart, but more often perfectly ripe. It was a lesson in risk and reward, he told me, because a perfect red apple was rare but divine.

"You don't believe me?" Tara asked.

Her words interrupted my memories. I stared up at her as I ate. Her arms were folded. She looked annoyed with me.

"I don't believe anything anymore," I said.

She hit a switch beneath the desk. The lights dimmed and a light turned on in the mirror behind me. It wasn't a mirror anymore at all, but a window.

"This is more how you imagined them, isn't it?" said Tara.

It was exactly how I imagined them. The room was crawling with limping, festering undead zombies. I wasn't shocked to see them. I expected them to exist. I took another bite out of my apple. Revelation swept over me. The sense of déjà vu returned, but with an answer. I knew this story, it was Dad's story and I was living it. The interrogation room, the shadowy government agents, the threat of zombies, all of it. I was so familiar with the story, I knew exactly what Tara would ask for next.

"This virus can cause the very apocalypse your father predicted," she said. "We have a way to fight it, but we don't have a vaccine. That's what we need. We need a cure."

"Is that all you need?"

Tara frowned at me.

"Yes. Lothryn, I need you to think. We can't find in your father's notes any clues towards what a cure might be. The antidote only wards off the virus for a time, but continued exposure guarantees death. Did he say anything to you? Think."

"I'm so tired of thinking," I replied.

"You're looking at test subjects exposed to the airborne pathogen. This is what happens to people. They die and walk around like husks."

"Why would you subject people to this?" I asked.

"We had to," she said. "This virus has come back to Earth clinging to shuttles of every space mission. Countries around the world can and will weaponize it."

I almost laughed at her agency's folly.

"But you'd like to be the first."

She narrowed her eyes, but she didn't answer me.

"I know he must have told you." she said. "Do you want everyone to die? We may be running out of time!"

"Time?" I asked. I considered where I sat, the physical bookmark in my father's story. "We're already out of time."

Tara's expression changed. I saw fear for the first time in her eyes. She said something in English and listened to a frantic voice chatter in her earpiece.

I felt unusually calm. I suppose I had reached a place of acceptance. I knew what would happen to the facility. I know it would soon be overrun with zombies. I knew what I had to do to survive. Dad detailed that to me in full.

"I'm surprised you didn't ask me about the most important part," I said to Tara. "How the outbreak happens. Dad used it as a lesson for me, to never do things that require concentration in an emotional state. Actually, Tara, it's all sort of your fault."

Her eyes darted to the mirror and back to me. Now I had gotten underneath her skin.

"Bullshit," she said.

I returned a tight-lipped smile and shook my head.

"Not directly," I specified. "But your actions specifically have consequences. You shot a detective, right?"

Tara didn't confirm or nod, but her scowl intensified and I knew it was true.

"She has a sister," I continued. "She works here. In Dad's story, she worked with my mother, but the fact remains that she handles this concentrated deadly virus. She's incredibly careful, of course. But today, she receives a heartbreaking message. Her sister, the detective, has been killed on duty. Your organization, being the kind of organization it is, requires her to work in spite of this. She has to develop the cure so you can create this super weapon. She's given no time to grieve."

Tara inhaled sharply. She kept looking to the mirror. I knew there were people watching me from the other side. She whispered something else with urgency.

"There's nothing that can be done," I said. "By now, it's already happened. She's gone back to work. Her hands are shaking. She feels like she's in a daze. She keeps remembering little random moments with her sister, a hug at the bus stop, an inside joke- things she forgot were actually so important. She can't shake the memories. A vial drops from her hands and shatters on the floor. It's hyper-concentrated and plumes like a cloud. She knows she and everyone in the laboratory are dead the instant it happens."

Tara's eyes were glassy. If she read my father's book, as she said, she knew I was telling the truth.

"And let that be a lesson, he would say:" Tara mouthed the words along with me. She was familiar. "Take time to feel better now, or you'll feel worse later."

I thought about the phrase. It really was some of his more sound advice. In fact, everything he ever taught me, I realized suddenly and truly applied.

"I guess he was a good dad most of the time," I said.

The lights changed in the room again, this time not from Tara hitting a switch. These lights were red and pulsing. A robotic voice began to speak over a radio system. Distantly, we began to hear gunshots and people yelling.

Tara's whole body was shaking. She stood and removed a pistol from her holster. She paced. it was odd to see her so devoid of confidence. She wasn't threatening, apparently, unless she was shooting from behind. Her voice cracked with panic.

"How can you just sit there? How are you so calm?"

I shrugged.

"I've heard this story so many times and I know what happens," I explained. "I'm going to live. You are not."

She snarled and pointed her gun at me.

"Fuck you," she growled.

It was English, but I got the idea. I wondered if I was wrong to provoke her. She did, after all, have a weapon in her hands. Maybe the story in action would be less kind to me. But she hesitated. Perhaps she felt she could still use me, or maybe someone told her "no."

She turned the gun away from me when a tremendous banging sounded on the door. I slid down beside my chair. Tara backed away with her weapon pointed at the door. The facility wasn't exactly built to survive excessive force. The old door was cracking under the weight of something strong and persistent.

In moments, the door broke down and two large, ravenous zombies fell into the space. They scrambled quickly to their feet and Tara began to shoot with wild, untrained aim. I tossed my chair into the mess and heard the gun clatter on the cement. She was easily overwhelmed and already dead.

I rolled to her gun and picked it up. My aim was better. I had spent years imagining just the scenario. I fired three successive shots, once in the first zombie's head, missed my second, but landed the third between the second zombie's eyes. My heart was racing with anxiety and yet, I felt somewhat vindicated.

Tara was bloodied and motionless on the floor. Her skin was torn from teeth and nails. The virus would find its way into her bloodstream and she would rise again.

I didn't hesitate. I pointed the gun and planted a bullet in her brain.

28. Hannah

"As soon as Erik died, we knew Lothryn would abduct you."

Perhaps if Hutch had said the words any earlier, it would have shocked me. But nothing shocked me anymore. I was face-to-face with a real-life zombie separated only by a narrow pane of glass. I could see every slimy, pulsing vein on his face.

"Well, not you in particular," said Hutch. "Just a girl between the ages nineteen and twenty-four within a radius of the apartment. It happens in Erik's novel with his characters Eramice and Sallas in some creepy male fantasy homage to Beauty and the Beast. Correctly identifying you was nothing short of a triumph."

I cringed as she discussed my abduction with any sort of positivity. And worse, I imagined that as Benton was shot and I was dragged against my will to Lothryn's apartment, one of Hutch's agents was watching and allowing it to happen.

"You might've noticed our collective of young, objectively beautiful women," she said. "We housed them in various locations around Lothryn's apartment. Our hope was that he would encounter one of them during his first excursion outside, but we knew that was a long shot. So as a failsafe, we place our agents on dating apps to bring them closer to other likely candidates. Tara found David. David led us to you."

She was too proud of herself.

"Sounds like you have it all figured out," I said.

"Almost," she replied. "We just need the cure. So tell me, Hannah Moreno, what do you know? What might've transpired between you two that we missed?"

It was hard to look away from the zombies, but I turned to face the bigger threat that stood behind me.

"You said that the reason I'm still alive is because I might know something that can help you," I said. "So if I don't know anything, you'll kill me. And do know something, you'll kill me after I tell you."

"Not necessarily," she said coyly. "If you show the potential for continued cooperation, I see no reason for your death at all."

Her face suddenly contorted to one of concern. She ran back to the deck and pressed the button on the mic.

"What was that?" She asked Tara. "What was that last part?"

She listened and sighed deeply.

"He's bluffing, he can't know that."

Then she sat, and she listened. I walked towards the two-way mirror that divided me from Lothryn and Tara. Lothryn's disposition had changed. He was speaking with new confidence. Tara was sinking into her chair. Whatever he was saying, neither she nor Hutch were pleased. Hutch began to turn through the pages of Erik Carpenter's manuscript. Her eyes were wide, intense, and wild with disbelief.

When Lothryn finished speaking, Hutch brought her hands to her face and massaged her eyelids. She reached for her pack of cigarettes. She nearly pulled another out of the box, but decided instead to throw the entire thing against the wall. I began to hear unusual sounds in the distance, a spray of bullets, concussive explosions, and shouting men.

"Damn it all," Hutch whispered to herself. She pulled a gun from beneath the table and stared at it like an old frenemy.

Red light began to flash overhead and an automated voice spoke over the loudspeakers.

"This is a red level alert," it said. "Environmental integrity has been compromised. Administering airborne EXtros antidote to the environment."

I heard what sounded like a stream of gas turn on. I didn't see anything, but the air smelled sweet like Tang. The automated voice continued.

"Please inhale deeply and make your way to exits in preparation for total lockdown. This is a red level alert."

Hutch stood up from her chair with the enthusiasm of a kid leaving the house for middle school. She walked past me to greet whoever was about to meet us at the door. The lock clicked and a pair of agents entered wearing masks over their faces. They both held guns.

"This better be under control," Hutch snapped at them.

"This took us by surprise, it's spreading fast and it's worse than we thought," said one.

"They've taken the courtyard," said the other. "Our exits are limited."

"Then stop talking and get us the fuck out of here!" Hutch yelled.

The agents nodded.

"Let's move!"

"Come on," Hutch said and she grabbed me by the wrist.

She pulled me back into the narrow hall. It was, without a doubt, one of the worst places I could imagine being in a zombie scenario. I had only watched a few zombie movies in my life. I wasn't an avid horror fan. But one thing that always got on my nerves was when characters made stupid decisions. And now, here I was being pulled down a poorly lit hallway with few options for exits. It would mean death if we were surrounded. I couldn't help but wonder if I would have been safer simply staying put and barricading the doors with the heavy desk and two chairs in the interrogation room.

And yet, I allowed myself to be led. Hutch and her agents had guns, I reasoned. I was foolish to believe they might actually protect me, even after hearing from Hutch herself that I was, in all likelihood, expendable.

The path twisted and turned, just as confusing as it had been going the other way. I was completely lost already, not that I knew where I was to begin with. Then I heard sounds racing towards us from behind, hisses, gurgles and growls that sounded anything but human. Hutch must've heard it too, because she turned and shot past me into the trailing darkness. The flash of her gunfire illuminated three or four disturbed and haunting faces. It was just for a moment, but we knew they were close and were catching up.

"Oh fuck!" the lead agent screamed.

And just like that, we'd been flanked. He fired his gun into the ceiling and emitted a blood-curdling scream as he was overwhelmed. I heard the footsteps of an approaching fiend and the grunt of a lunge. Hutch fired her gun again. I felt hands forcefully on my shoulders and I went down beneath the weight of my hunter. I thought I was dead. I felt the footfalls of other zombies trampling over me. Hutch's cries were drowned out by deafening gunshots.

But I was still alive. I hadn't felt the tearing of my flesh. I wasn't being devoured or torn apart. The body on top of me was inert. I pushed out from underneath it. There was dark blood in my hair, but it didn't belong to me. It had poured out of the zombie Hutch shot through the skull. Gunshots were continuing to blare, and I took off in the other direction, away from Hutch and the horde. I'd have to survive on my own.

I checked every door I passed as I ran. They were locked. I would need an appropriate keycard to gain entry. Finally, a set of double doors was open to my right. They were automatic but remained wedged open by a corpse that had fallen in the threshold. I leapt over it and continued down a section of hall that was glistening and white where it wasn't streaked with fresh blood and viscera. There was an exit sign at the end of the hall with glowing red letters. That was my goal.

"Hey!" I heard a woman's voice call to me.

She was seated beside a gurney trying to make herself small. I would've missed her had she not said anything. She was one of the pretty girls. One of her hands was on her neck, the other held a pistol pointed in my direction. I stopped in my tracks. She was crying.

"Let me leave," I said.

She shook her head and whimpered.

"There's no way out."

She pulled her hand away from her neck. It was bleeding profusely, an entire section had been torn out. Her teeth were stained red.

"Is it bad?" she asked me.

"Yes," I replied without mincing words. "Yes, it's fucking bad."

She returned her hand and scrunched up her face. She nodded to herself and the gun to her temple. Her blood sprayed against the wall.

I didn't have any time to process that horror. Rounding the corner, beneath the exit sign were two more zombies. I nearly turned on my heel, but I had the sense to reach for the dead girl's gun. I hadn't shot a gun before, but it didn't seem like there was an option not to. I turned and fired twice, landing a single bullet through the closer one's chest. He bled into his lab coat, but it didn't stop him.

So I booked it back down the hall. On my left, I spied a gray door without a keycard reader. The handle turned and the door opened. I slammed it shut behind me. I heard the zombies collide against it. But the door was metal and the latch held well.

I was in a stairwell with grated steel steps and solid cement walls. Blood dripped rhythmically from a corpse on the stairs. I could see it, lying motionless from two flights down. Other than that, it was remarkably quiet. Out of habit, I reached for my pocket. Of course I didn't have my phone. I hadn't had my phone since Lothryn took it.

I took a moment to collect my thoughts and take a breath. What a fucking mess. I occurred to me that it wasn't exactly helpful to stop and think about all that was happening. To do so was enough to send my anxiety through the roof and cause me to completely break down. It was better to block everything out and to focus on the simple task of escaping the facility.

After considering my options, I decided to go up the stairs. There wasn't immediate danger in sight, so I moved slowly and quietly. I held the gun out in front of me like I had seen cops do on television. I made it to the second floor, bypassing the dripping blood.

I was locked in the stairwell. The door on the second floor required a keycard. I cursed and looked up, wondering if the third floor would be so barring. I didn't necessarily want to ascend higher in a building I was actively trying to leave. The corpse caught my eye again. He was sprawled face-up with his head pointed down towards the landing. His neck was twisted. And he wore a black suit, so he probably had what I needed.

As I approached, I could see bite marks on his face and neck. It was probably similar to what I would have looked like had Hutch not shot my attacker. Attached to a clip on his shiny black belt, was his keycard. His name was Peter.

I crouched and reached for the keycard. It wasn't an easy thing to do from a distance. The clip was attached snugly. I jostled Peter a bit and finally freed it from his person. I pulled my arm back just in time to see his yellowed eyes open. My gun was already pointed at the top of his scalp and I fired. The bullet shot through his jaw and blood glugged out his skull like a twenty-four-ounce bottle of fruit punch.

I fell backwards towards the landing, dropped the gun, and hit my head on the railing. I gasped for air. He was a zombie, but it still felt like killing. I started to cry and I slapped myself to stop.

"Stop!" I repeated aloud. "Just get up! Keep going!"

I reached behind me and pulled myself up on shaky legs using the railing. I ground my teeth and bent to retrieve the gun. I looked back at Peter. He was motionless again.

His keycard worked on the second floor's door. It creaked as I opened it. I found another dark hallway. This one featured a few picture windows beside the closed doors. While it was nice to see any potential dangers that lurked inside the rooms, I knew it also granted any hostiles a chance to see me as well.

The first room on my left had rows of hospital beds. There were about twenty of them. Each one held a body. Each body had a bullet hole in its forehead. It seemed like a recent preventative measure. The glass was broken in the second room. A struggle had occurred. A woman was draped over the wall with the shards of glass piercing through her and a hole in the back of her head.

I could see a reflection of a monitor in the third window. I walked towards it. It was surveillance footage looking into Lothryn's living room. It wasn't a live stream, it was from before, when Detective Jarvis and Officer Clemmons broke down the door. I used Peter's keycard on the door and stepped inside.

I found a box of Erik Carpenter's belongings next to the computer. His dictionary was inside. With hardly a thought, I took it and placed it in the back of my shorts as I watched the feed. I saw David and Tara enter. I saw Tara walk casually into the hall. David was scared but he wanted to find me. Agents caught him off guard as they stormed the place. I watched us reunite. We embraced and I was escorted out. Then I watched as Tara Farris shot my best friend in the chest.

I reached and touched his body on the screen. He was a blurry shape on the ground.

Heavy footsteps race up the stairs. The door clicked open. I flattened myself beneath the desk and watched their shadows pass across the ceiling.

"Who the fuck let them leave?!" one was shouting. "They all got exposed! This shit's going to spread like a wildfire!"

"Do we got eyes on the boy?" asked another.

"He was spotted in the courtyard. We'll get 'em."

Their voices trailed off as their footsteps echoed down the hall. I felt the dictionary pressing into my lower spine. Why had I grabbed it? I think I knew the answer, even though it felt strange to admit.

If, by some miracle, both Lothryn and I survived, I wanted to be able to talk to him.

29. Lothryn

The lights were flashing red outside the interrogation room. The only other light was pouring in from somewhere above, casting an ominous shadow of a slow-turning fan. I would have to rely on the intermittent glow to learn from my surroundings. I appeared to have three options: the accordion door ahead of me secured by a padlock, the dark corridor I had previously been escorted through, or whatever lurked around the corner to my right.

Then, something happened that assisted my decision. Another zombie was lumbering towards me from the corridor. He was tall and skinny in only a hospital gown. I held my gun up and waited for the light to be its brightest. I adjusted as best I could, aiming for its head. The lights dimmed and rose again. It was closer. I readjusted and shot. I was pleased to see it go down.

I had to be conservative with my ammunition. Tara's gun was unlike my father's. I didn't know how it worked aside from the trigger. I guessed that I had around eight to ten bullets left. I didn't have the luxury of overestimating. I wished I had Dad's machete or katana. Any lethal melee weapon would do.

I turned to my right and headed around the corner. There was a ladder going up the side of the wall and the body of an agent beneath it. I knelt and searched him for a weapon. I found another gun beneath his shoulder and shoved it behind me into my belt.

The ladder led me on top of the interrogation rooms. The area was unfinished and crisscrossed with thick, wooden support beams. Far to my left, I found the small vent obscured by fan blades that made the shadows to my right. It appeared just the right size to crawl through.

I trekked towards it, weaving over and under beams and electrical cords. There were spider webs too. Dad told me about the two poisonous kinds in our area to watch out for: brown recluses and black widows. He said brown recluses liked clutter and dark musty spaces, like our apartment. He said black widows liked to build their webs in new wood like the beams of the facility. I considered the irony of being bitten and killed by a black widow rather than any of the immediate dangers of my current circumstances.

The creak of wood beneath my feet changed to a percussive snare of metal. I looked down and found myself standing on woven steel. I could see many bodies moving in the room below. I crouched and saw the zombies Tara showed me earlier corralled in their terrible testing space. A thunderous boom knocked me to my side and a flash of light spilled into the room. I heard cracking, falling cement. Dust plumed beneath me and the zombies ran out towards the light.

So much for their containment. A part of me was happy. They were once people unfairly tested upon. In death, they would have their revenge. Dad would have appreciated the poetry.

My ears were ringing, but I continued on towards the grate. I got closer, I could see that it didn't lead directly outside, but to a central courtyard in the building. I could hear people shouting and gunfire. It sounded like a losing battle. It sounded like the sound effects I had made in my own head every time Dad told me the story.

I kicked at the fan. It bent at the first impact and fell outside after six more hits. It hit the ground with a soft thump on a batch of dirt.

A bullet collided with the bricks beside me. I ducked low and peered carefully back out. I assumed at first that the bullet was directed at me intentionally, but from what I saw, that was unlikely. The courtyard was a vision of chaos. A woman with an assault rifle sprayed rounds into an encroaching horde; the upper half of a man was crawling with his arms with his intestines dragging behind him; a man screamed as he drove a golf cart mounted by a burning zombie and crashed through a glass wall. None of this surprised me.

I kicked my legs out and dropped down into the courtyard beside the fan. The landing stung my ankles. I rushed quickly towards a chain-link cage filled with boxes; it was my closely available cover. And yet, the space was already occupied. An agent was wrestling with a zombie. He pushed it back into the boxes before spinning around and seeing me. He had a shallow bite on his cheek. I shot twice. The agent and the zombie both dropped.

I stepped further into the cage to check on the status of the courtyard again through the chain-link. The woman with the assault rifle ran out of bullets and was overwhelmed, face down on the ground. The man in the golf cart was on his back, skewered with glass shards in a losing fight with a charred skeleton. Directly in front of me was the rubberized handle of what I discovered to be a shovel.

I shoved my gun into the front of my pants and picked up the shovel. It was weighty and the end was somewhat pointy. I wasn't sure how it would fare.

I left the cage with my growing arsenal and hugged the brick wall on the left side. As I ran, a pair of double doors opened in front of me. A woman was tackled through them and the zombie that landed on her proceeded to chew the back of its victim's neck. Another leapt out from the opening and I greeted it with a shovel to the face. It fell atop the others and I followed up, bashing its face less effectively than I would have hoped. It was too dull to slice and not heavy enough to truly smash. Instead, I stabbed straight down and pushed it deeper with the weight of my boot. I abandoned the shovel there.

An agent was running towards me. I heard his voice first. He was a large fellow with a shiny bald head. He had a gun pointed at me, but he wasn't shooting at me. They still wanted me alive. He shot intentionally behind me. He was trying to intimidate me. It didn't work.

I ran straight ahead towards a white pop-up tent. The agent gave chase even after I ducked into a crawl beneath the flapping tarp. I emerged in some small make-shift field lab beside a shelf stocked with glass and plastic containers. The man met me in the front of the tent and spoke with one hand on his ear. He assumed he had me cornered.

He kept his eyes on me and stepped closer. I side-stepped behind the shelf and pushed it on top of him. Glass shattered and liquid spilled. The man yelled first with shock and then with pain. Noxious fumes overwhelmed my senses and stung my eyes. I dropped to the ground and rolled beneath the tent. Something wet got on my sleeve and my flesh began to burn. I couldn't tend to whatever wound I'd inflicted, when I stood on the other side, there were three more zombies.

I pulled the gun from my back waistband. I fired once, twice, and, click, I was out of bullets. I threw the gun at the third zombie. It bounced off his face. But it bought enough time for me to pull my other gun and finish him off.

There was a half-open door beyond them. Semi-sheer bloodied plastic wafted out from the dark opening. I smelled smoke. I decided to run towards it anyway. I didn't see another viable option.

When I reached the door, I was caught off guard. It was silly of me to forget another detail from my father's story. In my defense, he didn't always tell it the same way. But occasionally he included a woman in a lab coat tackling him to the ground. That woman was the sister of the detective.

I saw the familial resemblance as she emerged from the darkness and took me to the ground. If I had been able to read her name tag, I would have known for sure she was Elaine Jarvis. Instead, I was focused on the pen in her front pocket. My gun had dropped and was too far away. The pen was my only option. I turned her onto her back and held her arms down with my knees. I grabbed the pen and took the cap off with my teeth. I grimaced as I brought it down like a knife through her eye. She went limp beneath me.

I retrieved my gun and went through the door. If Dad were telling the story, this was where he found my mother. She was helpless, surrounded by agents who were overwhelmed by zombies at the end of the hall. Dad fought his way to her. He saved her and then he lost her. It was all part of the epic tragedy.

That wasn't what I saw.

Down the hall, beyond a handful of zombies entangled with agents, was Hannah. She was on her own and firing a bullet into the head of an approaching enemy.

She turned to me, saw my face and she called my name.

"Lothyrn!"

It echoed towards me and I felt suddenly like I had a real reason to fight. I wasn't just living my father's story; Hannah and I, we had our own.

I bolted towards her. As I did, I saw an arm reach out. I ducked beneath it. I stood and fired a bullet through a face. I didn't know if it were a zombie or not. I just knew it wasn't Hannah. The smell of smoke became stronger as I got closer to her. I could see the glow of fire in her dark eyes. An inferno had taken the hall around the corner.

Hannah gestured up to my left. The stairs led to a mezzanine. I nodded and adjusted my path. Hannah followed after. The lower half of a man spilled down the steps. As I jumped over it, Hannah aimed up the steps at the zombie up top. She fired twice and ran out of ammo. I finished it off and ascended quickly.

My father's words went off like an alarm in my brain.

"Now, if you ever find yourself in this situation, you have to remember two things," he had warned me. "Never let anyone fall behind and always watch the stairs."

I turned back around. As Hannah followed me, a hand was reaching beneath the railing to grab her ankle. I made a hole through the zombie's temple. She jumped to the side and watched the predator fall. She shot me a look, grateful and understanding.

Along the mezzanine, we discovered the source of the fire. A young woman had a few bottles at her feet stuffed with rags. She held one in her hands and lit its rag with a lighter. She was about to toss it into the hall below when she saw us approach. She redirected her aim. I stopped. Hannah didn't.

I wasn't sure what to expect from Hannah. I had misidentified her repeatedly from the moment I met her. At one point, I concluded that she was a fellow survivor. That, as it turned out, was the most accurate of them all. She wasn't intimidated by the obstacle in our path who held an explosive fireball. She just kept running and bashed upwards with her shoulder. The waist-level railing was just low enough for the woman to tumble over the edge. She and the bottle hit cement with a spectacular eruption of flames.

Hannah put her hands on her knees and looked back at me.

"Damn," she said in my language.

My father's dictionary was shoved in the back of her shorts. I wondered if she had recently looked up the word, or if she was simply parroting something I had said a lot in front of her. Either way, I had to agree.

30. Hannah

When agents pulled me from the apartment, when I thought I was being rescued, I didn't expect I would ever want to see Lothryn again. I assumed I would, during legal proceedings sometime in the future. I'm sure I would have been disturbed by his presence in the courtroom. I would have helped to paint him as a bad guy in the eyes of the jury and the media. I would have testified to put him away.

That was before I learned the insanity of the truth.

In fact, the more my mind settled into the chaotic reality of what was happening around me, the more I was able to understand the reasoning behind Lothryn's actions. He wasn't the bad guy, his father was. Agent Josephine Hutch and her inhumane Project Delphi was.

I had followed in the footsteps of the agents that passed by the surveillance room. I knew I couldn't hide there forever. I smelled smoke and didn't want to risk burning alive while waiting for firemen to show, if they even would. I didn't know if I would trust any rescuers coming to my aide ever again.

I returned to what I believed to be the first floor. The smoke was thicker here and I could see the dance of fire alter shadows on the wall. More agents were fighting a losing battle against ravenous fiends. There were too many to stop them all. It was better to run. Perhaps the agents were under orders to make sure they eliminated any evidence of their mistake. That wasn't my problem.

A flaming zombie ran towards me. It didn't care that it was on fire. It just wanted my death. I shot a bullet through its face and the monster went down. I couldn't revel in my success, however, I had to look for an exit.

That's when my eyes locked with Lothryn's. He was standing in an open doorway about twenty yards away from me. Semi-transparent plastic sheeting billowed behind him from the frame like a cape. I flinched at first. It was hard to forget the fear I had learned. But I knew we could help each other, at least for the moment.

I called his name and a look of determination came over him. He began to fight his way towards me, but I knew we couldn't go the way I'd come from. Chances were, the path behind him was fucked as well. There were stairs to my right and I made it clear that's where we should head.

He reached the stairs first, but I saw another zombie at the top. I shot it in the shoulder and ran out of bullets. Lothryn shot it in the head. He was a much better shot, but I already knew that. Benton already knew that. I dropped my useless weapon and followed him up the stairs.

Then, Lothryn saved me. I wasn't sure how he knew to turn around when he did, but before I knew it, he'd shot a zombie whose arm extended in front of my feet. I would've fallen backwards down the steps like the agent I'd found in the stairwell. That would have been the end of me.

There was a woman on the mezzanine throwing Molotov cocktails to the lower level. She was one of the models like Tara who were there to be kidnapped by Lothryn or entice men like David. The very premise of her employment made me furious. When she saw us, she redirected her aim. I refused to be burned.

I played field hockey for a time in high school. I was frequently benched for unsportsmanlike aggression. I quit the team Junior year, but I still knew how to give a mean shoulder check. I didn't consider what would happen to the woman, I just wanted to survive and get past her. She screamed. I heard glass shatter and the whoosh of rising flames. Just like that, I had killed someone.

I planted my hands on my knees and took a breath. A word entered my head, something Lothryn had said before. I was pretty sure it was a curse word. I looked back at him.

"Hocha," I said. As swears went, it checked the box of being satisfying to say, especially if you emphasized the "Ho."

Lothryn nodded and ran to join me. I could tell he was impressed. I stood up and looked ahead. I had to look ahead. I couldn't focus on what I had done to get where I was. I could deal with that trauma if I escaped.

There was a closed door on the left. Lothryn reached it first and gave the handle a tug. It was locked. I held up the stolen key card. He smiled briefly and offered me cover as I used it on the card reader. Thankfully, the light turned from red to green and we were able to pass through.

It led us to a corridor that was mercifully quieter, if not eerily so. The floor was glossy, the walls and ceiling were matte, and everything was black, barring the vibrant red chair rails that seemed to guide us to the other end. It was how I imagined a modern-day vampire might decorate his lair.

I allowed Lothryn to lead me. With the gun in his hands, he was better equipped to react to oncoming assailants. He had a chemical burn on his shoulder where his skin had turned pink and blistered. It looked painful. He turned back to me and whispered.

"Hannah. Und byngyn."

It felt like an apology.

"It's okay," I said without thinking. I wasn't okay. I wouldn't be okay for a long time. But I needed him to keep his eyes ahead and my answer seemed to satisfy him.

There was no door at the end, just a black curtain made of heavy velvet fabric. It was so dark, I had to feel for a gap. Lothryn nosed his gun through first and I pulled the gap wider.

His face wrinkled with confusion. I poked my head in and understood why.

It was a large circular room with its tall walls completely obscured by the black curtain. A golden-tinted skylight made a cone of dim light. The ground was swirled with sand. Planted in the center was a dead and blackened tree. It looked similar to the logo I had seen on Hutch's binder.

There was a body on the ground beside the tree, unmoving and clad in a hooded red robe. As we crept closer, hearing the crunch of sand beneath our feet, I could see it was a man with a short beard. His neck was sliced through and a short silver knife was in his hand. I didn't even want to know the how or why.

"Oh great," I muttered, "Cult shit."

Lothryn shook his head. I wondered if he had any frame of reference for what he was seeing. Somehow, he looked like he had seen a ghost. He kept looking up towards the skylight as if he were expecting something horrible to descend upon us. But nothing did.

I crouched and recovered the dagger from the man's hand. His skin was cold.

"There's got to be another exit," I said to Lothryn.

I jogged over to the curtains and pushed against them. I felt around for anything that didn't feel like a wall. Lothryn appeared to get the idea; he ran to the other side and began to work towards me.

He called my name after a moment. His hand was pushing a section of curtain deeper than any I had felt. He lifted it up from the bottom as I reached him exposing an indentation with a rusty metal door with a crossbar handle. I pressed my back against it and pushed it open.

There was a garage on the other side with a few accordion doors and one side door with a glowing exit sign above it and a small window beaming in light from the outside. Lothryn and I were on a landing atop a short flight of steps. The black car I had arrived in was parked between up and the door. There were a few bodies on the floor, but they looked inert. I was more than ready to leave.

I gestured to Lothryn so he would take the lead again. We began to race down the steps and across the garage. The exit in my sights.

Then I heard a gunshot and I was falling. A searing sting was in my thigh. I didn't know what was happening at first. Lothryn turned on his heel and looked down at me, but he didn't rush to help me. His attention was drawn beyond me to the woman who shot me.

"Don't move," said Hutch.

I saw her, still bracing herself against the hood of the car. Smoke wafted from the barrel of her revolver. Blood was leaking from a hole in my leg. I felt more in shock than anything. My heart was racing. I was in pain, but my adrenaline was overwhelming.

Hutch stood and walked towards me with the gun pointed at Lothryn.

"Drop your weapon," she said to him and motioned with her wrist.

Lothryn complied. He crouched with his hand up and set it on the ground. She stepped out from behind the car. She was speckled with blood and limping. She had been through hell to survive, just like us. She made a sweeping motion with her foot. Lothryn nodded and kicked his gun away from him.

"So you can learn," she said. "This world is completely fucked now. If you're leaving, you're leaving with us and we are getting a cure from you if we have to literally pick it out from your skull!"

She continued to stumble towards me. Her eyes were locked on Lothryn. It was like I was completely unimportant to her. Lothryn held out his hands to her desperately.

"Tet hat ume fur go!"

Hutch rolled her eyes.

"What's the word for cure in your stupid goddamn language? Vora?"

"Tet pahtrel go. Lenshel ume!" Lothryn yelled back.

Her feet were planted right next to me. She didn't look at me. She redirected her aim at Lothryn's face.

"Give me a reason not to blow your brains out right here," she hissed.

Lothryn's eyes darted briefly to me. He saw the glint of silver in my hands. Then he replied, using words he had undoubtedly heard me use before.

"Fuck you."

If Hutch was indeed going to shoot Lothryn, I beat her to the trigger. The dagger was sharp and I slashed right through her Achilles tendon. She yelled and fired her bullet high before she buckled to the ground. As Lothryn rushed to retrieve his gun, I propelled myself onto Hutch with my good leg. I brought the dagger down and it sank into her forearm as she blocked her face. Her revolver loosened from her grip and I redirected it as she pulled the trigger.

Blood splattered against me and Hutch went limp with a wound in the side of her forehead.

I closed my eyes and fell off of her. I didn't want to look at her.

Lothryn knelt beside me. I reached for his arm. He put his hand on my knee. Every part of me ached.

"Von ume noya, indi gibber go wissahn," Lothryn said softly.

I could see his concern for me. I could see his heart.

"I know you're a good person," I said to him. "You were just so lost. And now..." I put my head on his shoulder. "Your heart's beating just like mine."

"Tsun- tsun gibber hadaersyn. Tet von secrah, doch ume-" He sounded panicked and he stopped himself. "Not here."

He looked through the window at the outside air. I got the impression that he was searching for some way to help me. Between the two of us, there was nothing to bind my wound. Everything was splattered with zombie blood. I was probably already infected. Hell, if the infection was also airborne, we both might've been.

"It's going to be chaos out there too," I said. "It might be safer if we wait a little inside."

Lothryn shook his head at me as if he somehow understood every word.

"Not safe. Not inside," he said.

He put my arm over his shoulder and helped me to my feet. With his pain jolted up my leg, but Lothryn helped me power through. I was awash with uncertainty. The fate of the world as I knew it was a black cloud.

Yet with Lothryn, I knew I had an unlikely ally. Together we pushed open the door and stepped outside into daylight.

00. David

My mother named me after her best friend. He died before the change happened. She said he was kind and loyal and always helped her when she had trouble making a big decision. I couldn't imagine that. Mom didn't ever seem to have trouble making a hard decision. She was tough and strong. She had a big scar on her leg from taking a bullet. She was my hero.

It took until I got older for her to tell me about the outbreak that changed life on Earth forever, not that I had anything to compare it to.

After she and Lothryn escaped the facility, they found their way to my abuela's apartment. They couldn't get out of the city. It was locked down and traffic was a nightmare. Though traffic was always a nightmare, Mom joked. So they boarded up the windows and camped out inside for a while. They drank EXtros to stave off the virus. Lothryn provided for them at first while Mom healed from her wound.

In time, they were both scavenging food and supplies, fighting off zombies, and keeping Abuela safe. Lothryn and Mom watched each other's backs. They had a special way of communicating, a special language that only they understood. She said they were an unstoppable team.

And yet one day, Lothryn was unlucky. He was caught off guard and got bitten by a zombie. He told Mom to kill him, but she tied him up outside. She flipped through the pages of their secret book. Folded into the back pages, on the back of a receipt, was a shopping list. Garlic, lemon juice, cinnamon, and ginger. At first, she didn't believe it, but she said she learned long ago that things she thought were ridiculous could sometimes surprise her and be the truth. She got the ingredients and mixed them together and it turned out to be a cure for the very virus that had decimated the world.

But it was too late to restore the world to what it once was. Mom had made peace with that. She said in some ways, it was a good thing. Plants and animals, for instance, were thriving. The virus didn't affect them.

She said Lothryn had a dream about building a community in the woods, something new and full of life. So Mom, Lothryn, and Abuela set off into the forest and began to build my home. They found other survivors like them, kind, hard-working people. Mom shared her cure, and the survivors shared their skills.

It took them a few years to get on their feet. They suffered through adverse weather, zombie attacks, and even a few altercations will fellow survivors. But what they built endured.

I was born into a nurturing community along with a few other kids my own age. We pick fresh berries in summer and swim in the lake nearby. We have a school. Sometimes Mom drives off with other adults and they look for other survivors. They usually return with new friends. They say the zombies are mostly gone, just corpses rotting in the sun. I've never even seen one. Mom says she hopes I never will.

She's never told me what happened to Lothryn. She said as close as they became, she couldn't shake the trauma she'd been through in his company. Apparently, they didn't start off on the best footing. Though she did say if not for Lothryn, she would have never met my dad. She said she discovered that Lothryn disappeared one day. And just ask quickly as he left, she met and fell in love with Isaac.

www.ingramcontent.com/pod-product-compliance
Lightning Source LLC
Chambersburg PA
CBHW072156070526
44585CB00015B/1173